MAN
TRIUMPHANT

By
ANNALEE SKARIN

DeVorss & Co., *Publishers*
P.O. Box 550
Marina Del Rey, Ca. 90291

ISBN: 0-87516-091-3

Sixth printing, 1977

Printed in the United States of America
by Book Graphics, Inc., Marina del Rey, California

CONTENTS

THE DIVINE SUBSTANCE OF DREAMS

Chapter I

The deep night of the ages is passing. The long sleep of the mortal regime is coming to a close. The awakening is at hand. It is the time for man to throw off the infant swaddling clothes of his earthly thinking and advance into the higher glory of divine thinking.

Man must now *know* that whatever he can think is possible else he could not think it. Man's very hopes and dreams reach out to stamp their imprint upon the elements of things "waiting to become!" By his pure, unwavering hopes man can gather those elements into tangible form. Such is the stuff of which man's dreams are made.

As man lifts his mind to contemplate the things that mortal eyes have never looked upon and views, in thought, the glory of the things unseen he begins to take hold of the creative elements of God. Such is man's power to lay claim to that divine "substance of things hoped for," and to weave it into tangible form, or to mold it into concrete reality. Man's hopes are the very essence of *"things that can become."* Those holy dreams, held out, as deep desires in a pure and yearning heart, must be fulfilled. Such is the law of God.

Holy, inspired hopes and thoughts and dreams come when one's mind is lifted to the very heights. They are heard by the spiritual ears or seen by the spiritual eyes of man as they are revealed by "The Holy Spirit of Promise, which the Father sheds forth upon all who are just and true."

Whatever man can think, or has thought, is already inscribed upon the invisible scroll of heaven. Man's very thinking transposes his thoughts upon that living record of eternity. No one can think a thought that will not be engraved upon the archives of "all-time." If one's thoughts are evil they are engraved eternally or until the individual himself repents enough to erase or recall them.

Good thoughts, high ambitions, noble aspirations are awaiting the fulfilling order of any who can believe and hold to their belief. A dreamer dreamed and then forgot his dream as he became engrossed in what is termed, "more practical things." In time he permitted the dream to fade from his mind and his heart as doubts took over his life. In relinquishing his hold upon his dream, through lack of faith, he gave up his right to fulfill it. Yet that dream remains a waiting promise for anyone who follows and who thinks those same thoughts again. Each time they are re-thought they are engraved more deeply upon the archived scroll of promise. It may be that they were thought many times before there comes forth the one whom faith and courage has fashioned strong enough to follow through—and so with power to fulfill.

As one holds to his noble dreams and aspirations he will develop the power to prove not only the reality of his thoughts but also the dynamic promises of God. When the power of the Almighty is linked with the living faith of man nothing remains impossible—or unfulfilled.

The very power to "believe" is the element of which faith itself is formed. And faith contains the substance of all things that are possible to hope for as man's mind opens to view the wonders of eternity. Thus the possibility of all existable things awaits the conception of man's thoughts and the patient nurturing of his emotions as faith fulfills the seed and brings it forth full formed.

This is the law of God. And this is the law of creation. And this is the wondrous power entrusted into the hands of man as he co-operates with God. This fulfilling is the power contained in God's Holy Spirit of Promise as it "promises all things and fulfills all things," through faith.

And so can be achieved all that man has designated as impossible.

Every day man is beholding the "impossible" dreams of the past coming forth into reality. The

twentieth century is the time when the impossible
is being brought forth into fulfilment as dreams
materialize into breathtaking realities.

But beyond the dreams of mechanical machines
and gadgets and financial gains and worldly wealth
and the outer realms of space are the inspired, personal dreams of individuals. These are the visions
which God has inscribed upon each human heart.
These sacred hopes contain the divine plan or pattern or sacred destiny of each individual child of
earth. When one opens his heart and soul to that
dynamic, inner call it becomes compelling and in-
sistent. Then it is that one becomes alerted to that
call that is like thunder as it vibrates into quickening within the soul.

When inspired thoughts or a divine revelation have
been engraved upon a stone, inscribed upon scroll
or written upon the pages of a book they become
known as "Scripture"—and therefore must be fulfilled. The Bible does not contain all the scripture
in the world, "for He shall speak to all nations and
they shall write it." "He shall reveal here a little
and there a little" "for the world itself could not
contain all the words Christ spoke had they all been
written" let alone the words that have been given
to inspired individuals, before and since. And because man bound those few inspired writings within
the covers of that certain Holy Book it did not place
a permanent seal upon the lips or upon the plans
of God that He can never speak again. It is true
that the promises contained within the Holy Bible

are God's words, and they cannot return unto Him void or unfulfilled. But God's words will never end as long as there are those who are willing to be taught and who have need of His instructions. "For they shall all be taught of God."

As His written words of high inspiration and divine revelation are picked up from a record, to burn anew within some searching, seeking heart, they are renewed and so revitalized. The power contained within them is henceforth increased by each rapturous rejoicing of an opened human heart. Everything that is written under the power of divine direction, whether in the Bible or out of it, is known as scripture. And anything that teaches a man to love and worship God and to pray is of God.

Be sure therefore that the word you read is not just some privately interpreted doctrine of narrow, creed-bound mortals. True revelation contains the exulting "Glory to God" ingredient as it reveals the vision of higher attainment—even the goal of perfection and of divine love.

Such divine, holy, exalting thoughts of praising love and glory and righteousness are the most sacred, divine dreams that God can share with man. These are also the holy dreams that man can share with God as his "eyes become single to God's glory." And so it is possible for man to begin to take on that same glory.

Any individual who will but take the holy words of God's promises into his mind and heart, and lay hold of them by living them, will assuredly receive the glory to which his soul is led to aspire, if he will but follow through.

Within man's being is the power to "PROVE all things and the ability to hold fast to that which is good." One can only prove all things by living them or by fulfilling them. And only as one lives the higher laws will he have the power to lay hold of them and prove them.

Professing words of proclamation are empty and an echoing mockery without the power to prove them. "His kingdom is not in word, but in power."

No promise is too great! No truth too divine! And no power can be withheld from him who lets God's holy promises stir into quickening as he lays hold of them with all his strength.

Such are the ties between man and God. And such are God's promises of things that doubting, mortal man proclaims to be impossible. He who thus seals himself into the gross darkness of unbelief will never realize that he alone has closed his own door to eternal progress and celestial light.

If man will only lift his eyes to behold the glory of God, with his vision single to that glory, he will KNOW that all things are possible (to him who believes). Such a one can never become lost in the dark blindness of unbelief. With his eyes single to the glory of God he must begin to take on and reflect that glory. To such a one nothing is impossible. He moves forward into that glory as he becomes clothed in the light his searching eyes behold.

Paul left this universal command for man's guidance, "Lay hold of the best gifts." What are the best gifts to you? Surely they are the ones which you are led to desire. The best gifts, to your mind, will be the holy promises that flame like neon lights of beckoning beauty before you, inviting you to leave the darkness as your open mind embraces such promises and holds steadfastly to them in eager, trusting hope.

Any gift that is desired, so that one may use it for the benefit of man, and not just to awe the minds of men, is most holy and divine. Such holy desires were placed within man's open heart by God Himself. And surely God cannot fail to answer the call which He Himself has placed within an individual's yearning soul or implanted in a searching mind.

Rejoice in every burning hope, in every noble desire, in every flaming promise of holy aspiration and know that as your mind lingers upon these things the pointing finger of "The Holy Spirit of Promise" is seeking to draw your attention to the things which were meant to become your own. Every divine promise ever given to man was sent out with "The Holy Spirit of Promise" sealed upon it and with the complete power of its own fulfilment.

At the first, casual glance you may doubt the possibility of His most dynamic promises ever being fulfilled in you, perhaps because you have known of none who have fulfilled them. If you have known of none who have fulfilled such wonderful promises then you should rejoice exceedingly, realizing that you are chosen as the instrument of proving. To you is given the greater opportunity to test and to prove His holy words as you are privileged to pioneer into new fields of everlasting glory.

To be the first to scale such noble heights is an honor indeed. It could be likened to the highest, unclimbed mountains of the world, waiting the centuries through for man to reach and climb and conquer and subdue as he attains the heights to which man never before ascended. No man can lift his vision to the inspired heights of promise who has not the power to achieve and to fulfill if he will but pay the price of putting all his energies and his strength into the conquest.

If man can, by desire and super-effort, subdue the earth and stand upon its highest, snow-clad pinnacles, know that no goal is too high for his searching soul to reach as his thoughts rise above the deep-worn valleys of human contemplation.

Man was created to subdue the earth, to rise and conquer every earthly condition and human trait. And the first and greatest of all human weaknesses the one of "UNBELIEF!" To believe one must go on to *prove* for he is required to *be* and *live* according to the vision his aspiring heart beholds.

It is always easier to settle back into the darkness of inactive dis-belief than it is to rise up and begin to exert one's God-given ability to believe, or to *be* and *live* according to the laws of Christ's Kingdom, which is not of this world. But he who exerts himself and who exercises his full power to live the laws will assuredly be given the power to evolve into that Kingdom.

Each man was created with a divine spark of God embedded within his soul. As that Spark, or Seed of God, is appreciated, "loved as a little child," and nourished by high and noble thoughts, it is quickened and begins its divine growth. It must be consistently fed upon the holy desires of exalted thoughts in the individual's own heart and mind. This desiring, this hoping, this believing is the very food of Gods. As this holy Seed is thus fed and nourished It "Grows and waxes strong!" This is the growth accredited to both John the Baptist and to Jesus Christ, Son of the Living God. This is the spiritual growth required for each individual's complete fulfilment.

As man grows spiritually, or as the Divine Seed of God, enfolded by a holy, immaculate conception within the very being of man, is quickened and brought forth, new visions continually arise to challenge his mediocre, trite, mortal thoughts. Such inspired vision must reveal the "Glory of God" and thereafter one's eyes become single to that glory.

Man, by the exerted power to believe, or to *be* and *live* according to the highest hopes and dreams he can possibly think, rises from the mortal level of conscious, grubby earth. He henceforth aspires toward the stars and new and higher vistas of increasing splendor continually unfold before his searching soul. As he lifts his heart to worship and adore and commences to live by every word ever released by "That Holy Spirit of Promise" into his soul, he begins to comprehend the divine glory of God in its fulness.

With this exalted vision established he will begin to comprehend that he is a very part of that glory, for as God Himself has said, "This is my work and my glory, to bring to pass the immortality and eternal life of man." If God's glory contains the immortality and eternal life of man then man is a part of that glory.

It is up to man to lift himself from the sodden bed of earthly thought and of the deep, stupid sleep of the ages. He must arise from the crib that has grown too short. He must cast aside the blanket that has grown too narrow, and with which he can no longer cover himself. He must awake from the indolent contentment and pacific lullabies of all earthly leaders as his soul begins to reach out and to grow into its full maturity.

Yes, "To whom shall God teach knowledge? And to whom shall he make to understand doctrine? Them that are weaned from the milk and drawn from the breast." Yes, Only those who are prepared to go beyond mortal instructions and who have advanced to the point where they can be "taught of God" can receive the full powers of their divine growth and maturity. These are the ones who have accepted Paul's instruction that they are to leave the first principles of the Gospel, or the milk, and go on to perfection. These are the ones who will "hunger and thirst after righteousness until they are filled— WITH THE VERY FULNESS OF GOD."

It is assuredly time for man to step out beyond the infant state of mortal thinking as he begins to aspire toward the challenging perfection held out to him by his Holy Creator. This divine reaching, this intense hungering and thirsting contain the only method by which one can possibly fulfill the measure of his own creation and so become a son—not only in word, but in deed, in goodness, in understanding, in love and power.

THE HOLY SPIRIT OF PROMISE

Chapter II

In order for man to comprehend fully the glory and the power of his association with God the "Holy Spirit of Promise" must be explained more fully.

The promise is and has always been, "If you will draw near unto me I will draw near unto you." Or, "If you seek me early you shall find me." Again: "If you seek me diligently you shall find me." "Diligently means to exert a constant effort to accomplish; industrious, assiduous," etc., according to the dictionary. And again, as God so graciously promised to all, "If you will abide in me I will abide in you." The above quotations remain only words, as do all of Christ's teachings, until they are proved by the living of them. "Live the teachings and you will KNOW."

"When thou prayest, enter into thy closet, and when thou hast shut the door, pray to thy Father which is in secret; and thy Father which seeth in secret shall reward thee openly."

This entering into thy closet means not only to find a quiet place to pray but to be able to close the door of one's mind to all outside disturbances and distractions. In other words, learn "To be still," by holding the mind and the emotions in complete quietude or silence. This place of deep, inner stillness is "The secret place of the Most High!" As one learns to "Dwell in that holy, secret place of the Most High," he learns to abide in God and then most assuredly will God take up His abode in that individual, even as Christ so definitely promised.

This "Secret place of the Most High" is the very center of one's soul as it is contacted by a conscious awareness. As one more and more learns to turn his mind and thoughts to this holy spot of high vibration and true enlightenment he will begin to be "taught of God." The messes and misfortunes and distresses and evils of his life will begin to be straightened out. The holy vibrations of that supreme contact can be released in power and the Father will begin to do the works, or work out all that is amiss, openly. This is the point of power.

It is in this holy spot or "secret place of the Most High" that the Holy Spirit of Promise is contacted.

"The Holy Spirit of Promise" is the very voice of God as high hopes are verified, holy aspirations established and divine thoughts are revealed and exalted into a clarified plan that necessitates fulfilment. Whenever one enters that secret closet of his own soul to hold "holy communion" with his Father upon any problem, project or subject and becomes "still", as he awaits his answer, he will be directed, informed or assured according to the need of the moment. And always that assurance and those promises so far exceed man's own bleak, little mortal ideas he will probably doubt, at first, the dynamic, breathtaking possibilities of their fulfilment.

After one has heard truth, or been instructed by this glorious, inner voice of promise, and believes in it and learns to trust it implicitly that individual will be "sealed with the Holy Spirit of Promise," as Paul declared in the first chapter of Ephesians. When one is sealed with that Holy Spirit of Promise, the promises given through that Almighty voice of God will be sealed upon the individual. And that seal cannot be broken.

Paul increased the knowledge of this power by explaining in the third chapter of Ephesians, the twentieth verse: "Now unto him that is able to do exceeding abundantly above all that we ask or think, according to the power that worketh in us." Or, to be more exact, according to the power of that Holy Spirit of Promise which we permit to work in us.

As one learns to abide in, or enter into this sacred, "Holy Place of the Most High," the gift of peace will become established. And this precious gift of peace will be the first that is sealed upon the individual as he learns to trust and to believe, though sometimes that Holy Spirit of Promise speaks most clearly and most emphatically out of a broken or breaking heart. It will often speak during moments of deepest despair. And in those moments, if one but lift his head and believe, the promise will be fulfilled no matter how impossible it may sound. And that answer will be made perfect. It is as one learns to listen—and to believe in those inner promises that they become sealed upon him and are forever established.

The voice of the "Holy Spirit of Promise" is infallible and though heaven and hell stand between that person and the promise given it will all be fulfilled—and more!

There is no question without an answer—and no problem without a solution. And God has them all.

And it is "The Father within who doeth the works," or works out those answers as one believes and permits Him to accomplish His works of fulfilling. The way for the individual to follow through, as God works out the plan, is accomplished by maintaining that glory of inner, perfect peace. It is in this inner quietude that God does His works.

Nothing that is revealed by the "Holy Spirit of Promise" is impossible! These inner promises of unimaginable beauty are the dynamic promises of the Almighty. They are not only possible, for all things are possible to God, they will be fulfilled to the very letter, or "To the last jot and tittle." It is as one becomes worthy of hearing that divine voice and believes in It that his life moves forward into a glorious state of fulfilment and joy. *"The Father*

*sheds forth the Holy Spirit of Promise upon all who
are just and true."*

If you do not believe this, then I am instructed
to ask you what it is that you have done, or undone, or left undone that you have shut yourself out
from this glorious, divine, wondrous voice of God
"That you might be taught of Him?"

These dynamic promises of Almighty God will
become verified accomplishments to those who learn
to hear That Voice and to trust in it, for it is the
voice of God, as it is shed forth upon all of those
who are JUST AND TRUE.

The holy Spirit of Promise is a priceless gift. It
cannot be bought with money. And often it is heard
most clearly when one has no money at all, for only
in this way can some become humble and teachable.
But destitution is not necessarily required for Its
loving expression of tender instruction.

One has only to learn to "Be Still," as he listens
to that inner instruction, in order to be taught of
God. And in that instruction comes an assurance of
well-being, of divine peace, of exulting joy, of complete, glorious satisfaction and of perfect understanding. This is the path of glory—"AND FEW THERE
BE WHO FIND IT!" It is the path Christ followed.
It is the pathway He left behind for each man to
travel who desires to rise above drab, ugly, mortal
existence.

In this divine contact one learns to trust implicitly
in every promise given and in every truth revealed.
And just by learning to listen, and to believe in this

holy voice of God, one advances into the great power of revelation and of complete KNOWING.

In this divine contact one finally learns to trust implicitly in every promise given and in every truth revealed. And just by learning to listen and to believe one advances into the great power of divine revelation. This is the coveted point all must eventually reach for the promise is that the day will come when no man will teach his brother or his neighbor, "For the day will come when all will be taught of God."

The perfection of this supreme method of divine teaching has been given several times in the scripture. Isaiah, the prophet gave it in these words: "And all thy children shall be taught of the Lord; and great shall be the peace of thy children." (Isa. 54:13). This precious passage of scripture was reaffirmed by Christ in these words: "It is written in the prophets; and they shall be all taught of God. Every man therefore that hath learned of the Father, cometh unto me." (John 6:45).

John, the Beloved also testified: "But the anointing which ye have received of Him abideth in you, and ye need not that any man teach you." (I John 2:27). This sacred, holy information is verified in the D. & C. Section one, by the holy revelation of God Himself.

This sacred method of inner, holy instruction is how God teaches. In this form of teaching there can be no error. Neither can there be false instructions given as one man takes upon himself the authority to direct and perhaps live the life of another as he usurps the rights of his brother, his neighbor or his associates.

Any holy promise that is whispered into the secret recesses of one's own soul, which is the sacred, Holy Place of the Most High, must be fulfilled if man will not doubt in his heart. This law of instruction and of revelation is so perfect and so complete and infallible there is no margin for error or failure, except as one refuses to believe. And these inner instructions are always exalting, glorious and sublime. They are never depressing nor doubtful nor evil. In this divine method, which God has reserved for a generation who ARE JUST AND TRUE, one needs only to rejoice in the privilege of walking with God in such a dynamic, holy calling.

In this divine, holy contact one must always be "JUST AND TRUE." It is quite necessary that one be just in all his dealings with his fellow men. He must be just in every act and every thought. This is the state of progress when, "One's mind and lips lose the power to hurt and wound," or to judge and accuse. One must be true to his highest flashes of inspiration and to the divine greatness of his own soul and to the holy revelations as they unfold to his understanding.

In order to advance fully into this Spirit of Revelation, as one prepares himself to be taught of God, he must reach out to God alone, trusting in Him implicitly and "lean not to his own understanding." And as long as one is satisfied with the method of being "taught of man" he will never have the courage nor the power to advance into this higher method of divine instruction.

The following is an exact pattern of the spirit of revelation as it was revealed over a century ago. "The Spirit of revelation is in connection with these blessings. A person may profit by noticing the first intimation of the Spirit of Revelation; for instance, when you feel pure intelligence flowing into you, it may give you sudden strokes of ideas, so that by noticing it, you find it is fulfilled the same day or soon; (i.e.) those things that were presented unto your minds by the Spirit of God, will come to pass: and thus by learning the Spirit of God and understanding it, you may grow into the principle of revelation, until you become perfect in Christ Jesus."

There have been those in the past, and there may be those in the future, who have taken the voice of their own evil lusts and earthly desires, as they have clamored for fulfillment from the wanton, satiated seat of their own mortal emotions, to be the direction of God. "Let no man say when he is tempted, I am tempted of God; for God cannot be tempted with evil, neither tempteth he any man. But every man is tempted when he is drawn away of his own lusts, and enticed. Then, when lust hath conceived, it bringeth forth sin; and sin, when it is finished, bringeth forth death." (James 1:13-15).

There need be no excuse for such errors and such deceptions. For "Everything that teacheth a man to serve and to love God, and to pray is of God." And anything that would injure another or trample God's

holy, divine laws of virtue and goodness into the dust,
that they might be passed over and ignored, is evil.

Also, "The Holy Light of Christ is given to abide
in every man who cometh into the world that he
might *know* good from evil." Therefore everything
must be carefully weighed and measured under that
holy light of inward knowing or instruction. Only this
divine light can reveal plainly the source of all new
information or reveal the truth or fallacy of old beliefs. In this infallible method one does not need to
be "tossed about by every wind of doctrine"—for
the "very truth of all things is given to abide in
man."

In this unfailing method one does not permit
himself to be deceived by his own lusts and craven
desires. He will have the courage to look at his weaknesses and to examine them under the intensified
rays of divine light. Then will he develop the courage to face his weaknesses and his lusts and with
this courage he will be given the power and the vision
to rise above them and to "OVERCOME."

To be instructed of God one must always be
"JUST AND TRUE." He must also be so filled with
love and reverence and devotion his own source of
love will be eternally enlarged and made perfect.
Such a one could not possibly be placed in the haz-
ardous position of listening to or lusting after evil
and then mis-thinking such cravings are of God. He
will love God more than he loves his weaknesses
and therefore he will begin to serve God instead of
the evils. This is the *overcoming*.

As one enters that "Holy of Holies" or "The sacred spot of the Most High" in true reverence and devotion, as he loves God with all his heart, mind, soul and strength, he will become so love-filled all personal lusts and wanton desires, along with all greeds and dishonest traits will be instantly placed in abeyance—

"The Holy Spirit of Promise" is the Spirit of Revelation in its highest degree of expression. Revelation itself may reveal disquieting conditions of the future, or of the past, or of the present. Not so the Holy Spirit of Promise. It reveals only a pattern and the promises of exulting, glorious attainment. It is the divine method of personal instruction and promise to the individual. This divine voice is always peaceful and breathtakingly beautiful. It reveals the almost unspeakable promise of one's own happy, divine fulfilment. It is the loving voice of God as it unfolds the sublime pattern God planned for that individual's progress and happiness along his own pathway of divinity. It contains always the deep inner peace along with the joyous, stupendous promises of eternal good. It always carries the message of divine assurance that "all will be well," no matter what outside condition may prevail. It bears witness to the soul and to the mind of God's most holy promises as it establishes the method of their fulfilment. And through one's opened attention God's power is permitted to begin its fulfilling works of completion, or of bringing forth, or of allowing "God to do the works."

"The Holy Spirit of Promise" truly promises all things. And united with the principle of faith, FUL-FILLS THEM. As one gives heed to this voice nothing is impossible!"

As one becomes JUST in his dealings and in his thinking, and TRUE to his own highest instincts and thoughts and to the divine vision contained within his own soul, that Holy Spirit of Promise will begin to bear witness that God approves of him. "As one continues to humble himself before God, hungering and thirsting after righteousness, and living by every word of God the Lord will soon say unto him, *son, thou shalt be exalted*. When the Lord has thoroughly proved him and finds that man is determined to serve him at all hazards then the man will find his calling and election made sure."

In Hebrews the eleventh chapter and the fifth verse is given this information concerning Enoch of old: "By faith Enoch was translated that he should not see death; and was not found, because God had translated him: for before his translation HE HAD THIS TESTIMONY, THAT HE PLEASED GOD."

In this divine approval it is the "Holy Spirit of Promise" that will bear witness to the individual that he is chosen or approved as it reveals day by day the pathway of fulfilment.

As one gives heed to those inner directions he will finally receive the Second Comforter spoken of in John the fourteenth chapter. This second Comforter "Is no more nor less than the Lord Jesus Christ

Himself. When any man obtains this last Comforter, he will have the personage of Jesus Christ to attend him, or appear unto him from time to time, and even He will manifest the Father unto him, and the visions of the heavens will be opened unto him, and the Lord will teach him face to face, and he may have a perfect knowledge of the mysteries of the Kingdom of God."

Those who develop that "hungering and thirsting after righteousness" must begin to be fed by the direction of that inner voice of God until they are prepared to behold His face. Within the contact of that Holy Spirit of Promise, which the Father sheds forth upon ALL who are *just* and *true,* His divine promises are all intensified and personalized to apply to the individual as his own pattern and needs are unfolded and revealed. As one holds to these promises, or "lays hold of them" as Paul admonished, their fulfilment must come and God's power becomes established. And then it is that the divine promises become SEALED upon the individual as he advances into a complete KNOWING. Then it is possible for him "to receive the great and last promise, EVEN THE UNVEILING OF THE FACE OF GOD."

Blasphemy you say? Not so! Christ never spoke blasphemy and these are His words. Only man's life has contained the great blasphemy of the ages as he has dragged along in the gross darkness of unbelief and unprogressiveness.

I have been commanded to write these eternal

truths and to reveal the powers connected with them. *It is possible* "For man to evolve from the man kingdom into the God kingdom!" But man himself must do the evolving. And the only thing that is utterly *impossible* is for any one to do this evolving who is satisfied with himself just as he is—and with mortal conditions just as they are. And be it here known, that it is always the most mediocre individuals who are satisfied with themselves and who therefore refuse to make the effort required to even begin to evolve or progress beyond earthbound conformity.

Into your hands I am commanded to place these sacred, divine keys that the way of overcoming be now yours—and the road of eternal, joyous, everlasting, wondrous fulfilment as you begin to take upon you His Name—and His powers—if you so choose.

THE LAW OF THE ANGELS

Chapter III

The law of the angels is that they must do the very best they can upon every occasion and with every assignment and at all times. Their second best will never do.

This is an open law that can be lived by every mortal on this earth who desires to live it: And by accepting it and believing it one will be lifted into a higher status of advancement.

To apply this law of the angels in one's life demands that all careless living be left behind for in every casual, inconspicuous act the law must be employed. No slip-shod habits can be tolerated under this law. And it is amazing how quickly the law, when applied, develops a meticulousness of character and habits that is irreproachable and quite natural of execution. Under its application slovenly actions and careless, often shameful little hidden, sneaky traits are soon eliminated.

One automatically develops a degree of self-respect which demands his best at all times. Under this law he begins to live up to the inborn goodness within himself. He also develops dignity, poise and a deeper compassion for those with whom he comes in contact. And as poise increases it expands into majesty as the law of performing every act as perfectly as possible is fulfilled. And majesty is the manifestation of the law of divinity. Only one's best becomes acceptable to the individual who takes hold of this divine, higher law and lives by it. His second best is never good enough as one begins his upward march toward ever higher goals as new standards unfold before him and are themselves reached in fulfilment.

It is true that such a one will become a "perfectionist." But he will only be demanding perfection of himself, not of others. In his own efforts to always do his very best he will find a satisfaction. He will also find the method of his own growth, happiness and fulfilment.

As one applies this law in his life his mortal, negligent, thoughtless, careless and often reckless and harmful actions become intolerable. As he applies the law it soon becomes a very part of himself—his wonderful, advancing SELF.

It is a beautiful law when lived. It holds the keys of dignity and of charm and of true nobility. And any who will live this law will have the recognition of the angels and will be assisted upon every occasion in fulfilling it and in perfecting themselves.

This divine law of the angels is really the law of man's innermost nature. It is the law of himself as he opens up his soul to the fulfilling of himself. By applying this divine law in his daily life one soon comprehends the satisfying, rewarding power of its miraculous beauty for it brings its own rewards.

My father, who was a very wonderful man, died when I was nineteen. He approached his end after a long, lingering illness. It was just a few days before his death that he called in his children, one at a time, to extract from each a very noble and exacting promise, according to his love and wisdom. And I alone, of all the children, could not make that promise. To me a promise was a most sacred obligation. I realized fully that if I made that promise I would be bound by it all the days of my life even if the years ahead proved it to be erroneous and harmful.

I was greatly distressed as I looked into my father's expectant eyes. I would have given my life to have made his last hours more happy and serene, but I felt that it was more than my life that was at stake. It seemed that a knowledge deeper than his wisdom and understanding and far beyond my own forbade me taking such an oath. With deepest regrets I answered, "I cannot make that promise. I can only promise you that I will do the very best I can all the days of my life."

I did not realize it at the time but by that promise I was forever bound by a higher law and a far

greater promise than my father had desired to extract from me. I had unknowingly taken an oath
to live the law of the angels.

It took me years to grow into it. But it was in
the living of that law that I found the divine wonder
of God's love. It was in moments of dynamic fulfilling of the law that angels came at various times
to minister unto me.

In looking back I realize fully that had I made
and kept the sacred promise my father desired of
me it would have ruined my life and would have
closed the door to the fulfilling of my destiny. I
would have betrayed myself and God also. By the
promise my soul was prompted to give I have grown
to rejoice in the law of the angels and to understand
it perfectly. I have learned of the sublime wonder
and unfolding glory held within its depths. I have
learned to love this law, which alone, can bring
complete attunement with God and the divine powers
of heaven.

Gradually the conscious awareness and the effort
to fulfill the promise I made to my father became
a part of my existence. I finally reached the point
where I never had to give it a thought, though it is
a law which requires conscious effort and awareness
at first. Then, as one grows into it the very strength
and powers of heaven are released into his life. And
that life becomes an ever increasing melody of advancement. The law of the angels is the first law of
heaven. And all that is required is that each one
live it according to his own strength and under-

standing. But live it he must if he would attain unto the heights.

As one takes hold of this law and begins to apply it in his life, he may find, to his consternation that his best is not nearly as good as he had always thought. His best, no matter how good will need much practice to bring perfection. It is like the woman who, every morning, refused to let her small son dress himself. He would cry and plead for the privilege of putting on his own clothes and lacing his own shoes and with inconsiderate impatience she would brush his pleadings aside because his best was not acceptable. She did not realize that his best would increase into better and that only by doing his best, though imperfect, could he possibly grow into perfection. The pattern of his life was thwarted for many years because his childish best was not acceptable.

This law of the angels is one of natural fulfilment as one's best increases day by day into a fuller more abundant life as newer and higher goals and powers continually become manifest. This is the law of perfection and one must grow into it as he develops his abilities.

It was a long while before I understood how powerful and far-reaching was the promise I gave my father. He had not intended to extract such a promise from me and I realized, at the time, that he was disappointed in my failure to accept his terms of life. But all the days of my mortal life—

and beyond—the gratitude I have for that promise
I made, sings in my soul.

To live the law of the angels was a far greater
promise than my father had requested, though he
realized it not.

This higher law demands, even when one is eating
alone, that he eats with the worthiness and dignity
of partaking of a great banquet attended by many.
And though the meal is humble, and though the fare
is poor it will be a banquet and angels will attend.

If, in every personal, private act one lives according to the highest laws possible for him to fulfill,
from the point where he stands, he will never be left
forsaken and alone in time of need.

If, in every public action and every required assignment, one performs his task as though it were
a divine obligation it will become just that and be
crowned with the approval of heaven. And even
when he thinks he stands alone he will be standing
in the presence of divinity and angels will rejoice
over him.

Such is the law of the angels and such is the
law of man's innermost being, for it is the law of
"The Kingdom of Heaven," which is within.

He who lives this law will soon learn of its power
as he grows into it.

One does not fulfill this law in an instant. This
law must be lived in order to develop graciousness
and that true, inner worth that eliminates disreputa-
ble, debase, careless habits. This law is a law of
beauty and power and divine attainment. It is a

law one must, of himself, elect to fulfill. It can never be forced upon one. And as one lives the law it becomes his own. By applying it in his life he exalts himself into a higher vibratory existence in which the angels may be called to attend him in every moment of need and during periods of unusual performance, for he will continually grow into more and more dynamic situations. Upon those extraordinary occasions, when much more than usual is required, he will know that angels are there rejoicing over him and lending their strength to his to fulfill the appointed task.

This is a sacred, wonderful law to live by, and to fulfill. And as one lives it his power to perfect and to glorify increases. "That which you persist in doing becomes easy to do, not that the nature of the thing has changed, but your power to do has increased."

In living this divine law of the angels one can never let himself or another down. Neither can he be caught in some humiliating, shameful act or circumstance. His whole life develops into an harmonious procedure of purest joy and honor as he grows into the use of the divine powers of heaven.

The laws of the land and all secular, mortal laws, to which one may conform through his chosen, earthly adherences, requires no such meticulous, astringent compliance. All the laws of the creeds demand only the cleansing of the outside of the cup, for they contain only the outside, temporal laws and mortal regulations. These higher, inner laws, when lived, clean not only the outside of the cup but the inside as well for they are inner laws. And they are chosen and performed through a complete willingness to do all that is required—and a little more. They must be selected and accepted by the individual who enters this higher order of existence. This law of the angels is not a compulsory law, but it is a law that pertains to that straight and narrow path which so few find—and are willing to travel.

On their assignments of service and love the angels are sent forth to assist all who call, or who are in need. Yet the person or group to whom they are sent may never acknowledge or know or even accept that assistance. This is the law that supercedes that continual demand to be appreciated. In this law one never works for the worldly pay of appreciation. It is the law of doing one's very best in every circumstance and upon every occasion without a thought of reward—even in thanks. And though the angels may be actually rejected in their assignment yet it does not change their law in the least. The angels are still required to fulfill their law of loving service *to the very best of their ability.* Of them it is required that each must send out the very highest vibrations of love and healing power that is possible for them to generate, collectively or individually, though this is the law of each individual.

This is not the law to be seen of men. This is the innermost law of man's own being. It is the law by which man grows into his own highest possibilities, subtlely, unnoticed and unacclaimed, yet dynamically, eternally powerful.

This law is power. And as one begins to live by it his power to do will increase until all perfection is attained. The aspirant must live according to his highest, inborn ethics. From the moment he takes upon himself the marvelous wonder of this journey toward higher goals he can never again stoop to do little, underhanded, slovenly things or perform sneaky little actions in the hope that he might be able "to-get-away with them." Every little spiteful act and vengeful thought must be eliminated as one fulfills the law. In this law love increases and understanding compassion becomes the power of existence. And the Second Great commandment will be fulfilled, naturally and beautifully.

No one on this earth, or in the universe, for that matter, ever "gets-away-with" anything that is unworthy of himself. In striving to put across some unworthy or dishonest act one first of all fails himself. And in doing so he places himself upon the lower level of deficiency and stamps himself with the seal of mediocrity. He may even place the seal of the "animal status" upon himself. And there are those who sink even lower—below the level of animals.

Each and every unworthy, inferior action places its seal of inferiority upon the individual as the higher laws of his own glorious fulfilment are rejected and ignored.

The divine gift of free-agency, so graciously bestowed upon man from the beginning, gives him the right to select the kingdom he will inhabit and the type of individuals, who are like unto himself, as eternal associates. Each individual selects his own kingdom or realm or level by his compliance to the laws pertaining to that level. Thus it is each man's right to reach upward into the realms of eternal light as he fulfills the greatness of himself. Or he can degenerate into the lowest state and become even less than mortal in his bestial habits and unworthy actions.

The laws are his own. They always have been.

The law of the angels is always there waiting, like an engraved, gilt-edged invitation to enter the higher realms if one so desires. And no matter how lacking one is, or how insignificant or deficient one can begin to increase his power and goodness and mercy and understanding by living according to the highest laws of his own inner nature. By living the higher laws one must increase in joy and virtue and beauty and the divine power of his own fulfilment.

The priveleges of heaven and the sublime, infinite powers thereof are held out continually to all who will only accept them and live by them.

As one lives by the higher laws he automatically proves them, not only to himself but to all with whom he associates. "Live the laws and you will KNOW of their truth." And "knowledge IS power." It is by living the higher laws that all things become subjected unto the individual for the promise is: "And all things will become subject unto you, both in heaven and on earth; the light and the life, the Spirit and the power."

What greater promises could be given?

This is the promise of God as one begins to fulfill his own divinity. And the laws pertaining thereto are man's to apply in his life. They are his to grow into, to rejoice in "as he evolves from the man kingdom into the God kingdom."

And they are yours. If you doubt ask God to help your unbelief. If you are weak ask Christ to give you strength.

These books have been "Written by the finger of God," as the author of the Odes of Solomon proclaimed. And that finger has been held out to you that you might take hold of it and stand upright to view the wonders and the desirability of the higher realm. But this work is only to give you the vision. It is up to you to take your own, perhaps faltering steps, alone. No one can take those steps for you. Neither can another walk this divine pathway for you. The journey is your own. And it is as different from the present, mortal estate as the crawling position of an infant is beneath the achieved advancement of the child who has learned to stand upright and to walk.

If it seemingly takes too much effort to break through the confining shell of your complacency then you must remain in your infant crib of conformity and unprogressiveness. You will be required to continue sleeping in the crib that has grown too short for you to stretch yourself in, with the covering that has become too narrow for comfort or warmth. If you are content with this condition, and with a milk diet, or worse, the banquet of vomit, then no one can help you.

It is a painful, harrowing experience for a child to be weaned from the milk and drawn from the breasts. But for development it is a necessity. It is also an anguished experience, taking those first trembling, doubtful steps. Yet in that achievement is contained one of the great triumphs of a lifetime. I know, because I remember. Those fearful, halting steps exalt the baby from infancy into childhood. And it takes so few of them to give the child confidence and the proficiency to go on thereafter, upright and eager to meet the challenge of life.

And it takes only one step at a time to begin traveling along this higher, spiritual road as one begins to apply the law of the angels in his life. Each act one performs, and usually one only performs one at a time, he can use the law, even as step by step he learns to walk.

It is only by one's own exertion that he can possibly grow into the full stature of himself—a child of the Most High God.

Come, beloved, the way is your own. Just do your best, always! And if you fall, help will be sent to assist you until your feet are planted safely and surely upon the way that leads to your own divinity.

JESUS CHRIST,
SON OF THE LIVING GOD

Chapter IV

The way of inner promise and lighted instruction is the path Christ followed in His exalted life of supreme service. He proclaimed that He spoke no word save His Father commanded it and performed no act except God revealed it. This was not only the point of His high attainment but the point He coveted for all. When He spoke of this degree of inner directing He was not boasting about something He alone could achieve or had achieved. He was revealing the way of possible attainment for every child of earth.

Christ, through perfecting the ability to "be taught of God," had advanced so far He would have automatically been transformed into the fullness of His divine stature and heritage and would have thus been exalted beyond the vision and physical reach of His followers without them in any way comprehending what had happened. For that very reason Christ chose and accepted the way of the cross. He desired that all should see and comprehend the higher laws and possibility of perfection and the powers thereof—even the power over death itself.

And for centuries the world has held its attention upon that shameful betrayal and the shocking horror of His death. Men have tried always to keep alive the anguish they would have suffered had they been in His place. Man has always sought to bring God down to his own level. In portraying only Christ's suffering they have held His supreme sacrifice upon a mortal level of humiliation and dishonor.

It is true that on the last night of His mortal life, as Christ kneeled alone in the Garden of Gethsemane, while His followers slept, He sweat blood. And the world, in its ignorance and blindness, has believed that Jesus so dreaded the ordeal of the crucifixion He sweat blood through His personal fears and anguish.

No mortal idea could be more false than this.

As Christ first kneeled, before His followers dropped off into an exhausted slumber, they heard His words, "Father, if it be possible let this cup pass from me; nevertheless not my will but thine be done."

As Christ completely relinquished His will to the Will of God, His Father, He was shown the history of the world—all that had been—all that existed in His own time—and all that would be in these far off, distant years of ours. He beheld all the errors and mistakes, all the weaknesses and evils, all the sins that had been and would be committed under ignorance, blindness, determined wickedness or sanctimonious self-righteouness. He comprehended the darkness and the defiance, the bigotry and the secret sins of a lost world. And in that revelation His heart melted in a compassion so great His physical system could not endure the divine grandeur of His love. His very blood oozed through His pores as He yearned over the sinners of a world so engulfed in ignorance and self-imposed blindness and so cloaked in hypocrisy His suffering reached beyond mortal minds to comprehend.

Christ realized fully that all the pain and anguish and suffering and dismays that could or would exist were caused by the rebellion and ignorance and the consequent evils released through the lives of men.

In beholding the great drama of the world Christ saw every living soul. In that vision He beheld your mistakes and mine. He viewed the weaknesses we held secreted within our hearts, sins which we concealed behind our human, mortal personalities. He beheld the transgressions and the errors of every living soul and the tragic, hunger crying out of each individual's innermost being as he reached instinctively for a better way.

He comprehended fully that the distresses and afflictions of the world and its almost unbearable sufferings were caused through the mortal weak-

nesses and blind evils of humanity. He beheld that
mankind had no idea as to the cause of its distresses and even a great ignorance of what to do
about it.

In that all-encompassing revelation Christ's heart
opened wide to enfold the world completely in His
own divine, God-like love. His soul yearned with a
yearning no mere mortal mind can possibly comprehend. With an almost consuming desire He pleaded
with His Father to be permitted to help atone for
the evils that had become the heritage of man. It was
in the burning intensity of His desire to help atone
for the gross wickedness of all the ages that His
mortal blood was almost drained from His body before ever the ordeal of the cross arrived.

If only His disciples had remained "Awake for that
one hour" they would have comprehended, in a
measure, some of the divine, unspeakable wonder of
His greatness and His love. But they did not stay
awake. They slept as most of mankind is still sleeping today. They were only awakened in time to behold those drying drops of His life fluid still upon
His face. And it was they, who later assumed, that
His anguish had been caused by his own fearful,
cringing dismay at the ordeal before Him.

Because they had not remained awake they failed,
for the time being, to comprehend the great glory of
His sacrifice and the divine power of His love. Because they had slept, as most of us have done—and
are doing, they were unable to understand that His
yearning for them and for the entire world was so

acute and so profound He would gladly have sacrificed His life a thousand times upon a cross. He,
in that hour of divine anguish, could think of no
price too great to pay for the redemption of a world.

It was not for Himself He sweat His precious
blood. It was for us. And it was for us He died.

It is now "the fulness of time" and that which
has never been told must be made known.

In Christ's ardent, concentrated desire to offer
Himself for the sins of the world, His own ordeal
became as nothing.

Many of us, who were yet unborn, were there to
behold, in sorrow, that ordeal and to rejoice in His
dynamic victory. We understood its meaning and its
glory as we worshipped and adored. And with all
the strength of our souls we sought to return to Him,
in a measure, His great love as it penetrated our
beings and poured out through us. Our love fell short
else we would have remembered the great wonder
of His sacrifice when we first heard of it again in
the story of Christianity and the betrayal of the Son
of God and His death upon the cross.

In reading this many of you will recall the great
truth behind His sacrifice and remember that none
of His suffering was for Himself—but for us. And
your love will be deepened by that knowledge.

To Christ the great ordeal became as nothing in
the urgency of humanity's great need. And so can
every mortal ordeal be overcome, transformed and
exalted. It was by this singleness of "Praise be to
God" that all martyrs were exalted above their mo-

mentary tortures and afflictions—and above their cruelly inflicted deaths. They too became detached from all personal suffering through a devotion that completely suspended the self and superceded the physical claim.

To Christ, our Lord, the supreme sacrifice was a divine privilege. It was not an ordeal, as man would interpret it. He so exalted and transformed the shameful experience into an act of everlasting glory there was no other thought or feeling in His mind. His very singleness of purpose perfected His divine heritage and exalted His mortal body into divinity. He was so filled with love and light and the high purpose of His desire that when the multitude approached Him in the Garden they were momentarily overcome by the power of God He held out to them in His infinite love. He was so filled with the light and the glory of eternity they were almost paralyzed by it as He towered above them in His own divine majesty.

Throughout the mockery of His trial, the indignities of His persecutions, and the crowning dishonor of thorns and the discreditable, ignominious ordeal of the cross He never, for even one moment, flinched, nor faltered nor cringed. He never for a single instant acted less than He Himself WAS, the divine Saviour of the world. Majesty crowned His every thought and the vibrations he released were sent out only in love.

He never asked for pity nor sought for sympathy. As He dragged His cross along the streets of old

Jerusalem, He was also dragging all the crosses of all mankind, as individuals would in time, yield them up to Him. It was the crosses of all the individuals of all the ages that made a weight so heavy He stumbled under the burden of it. In carrying that cross He was calling to all the over-burdened of the world, "Come unto me all ye who labor and are heavy laden and I will give you rest. Take my yoke upon you for my yoke is easy, and my burden is Light." His burden is truly the great Light of heaven, the Light of glory, the intelligence and truth and power offered to every, humble, searching soul. Yes, His yoke is easy. It was our yoke upon Him that was so heavy on that tragic day, so long ago.

Christ still holds out the wondrous burden of the great Light to every child of earth who will only desire it and accept His divine offering.

And, as Christ went along that dusty street "There followed Him a great company of people, and of women which also bewailed and lamented him."

But Jesus turning unto them said, "Daughters of Jerusalem, weep not for me, but weep for yourselves and for your children."

The self-pitying anguish portrayed by the mortal, morbid-minded imaginations of artists are but revealing their own level of reactions had they been called upon to endure such an ordeal in their sin-drenched, self-centered, human weaknesses. Had they been called to endure an experience as disgraceful, as humiliating and as anguish-filled as that crucifixion they would most assuredly have looked and felt as pitiful and undignified as they depict Christ being. And in their shameful portrayal they "crucify Him afresh" adding to the first shame their own evil interpretation of the event.

In the hours of His ordeal Christ was never for one moment anything less than the divine Son of God, as He had testified from the beginning.

His divinity was proclaimed anew in His compassionate words of tender love as He pleaded, "Father, forgive them, for they know not what they do." He was willingly offering up His life for the sins of the world, "No man could take his life from Him. Of himself he could lay it down, and of Himself He could take it up again." Which was incomprehensible to those who heard until He proved His words by His ascension from the tomb.

During that suffering on the cross Christ never forgot for a single instant the urgency of His sacrifice nor the purpose of it. Nor were any excluded from His love nor from the benefits He held out to the world. It was for those who had committed the most appalling crime of all existence that he pleaded, "Father, forgive them" and then gave an excuse for their crime. Tenderly, sincerely and with nothing but love and forgiveness in His heart he prayed for the blasphemous wickedness they had perpetrated to be blotted out.

Should any feel shut out from His mercy? They need only turn to Him in earnest entreaty and He will hear. Should any man think he has sinned too much to be forgiven? No one has sinned too much until he has lost the power and the desire to ask to be forgiven.

Such is the healing, enfolding mercy and the power of the divine love of Jesus Christ, Son of the Living God.

Even at the very beginning of Christ's betrayal He lifted His head in humble triumph, saying, "Now is the Father glorified in the Son."

The erroneous mis-translation of His words, spoken from the cross, still stand in jeering mockery, "My God, My God, why hast thou forsaken me?" This has been the crowning insult and the second greatest falsehood.

His words were: "Eloi, Eloi, lama sabachthani," which being interpreted by the mortal minded, who stood by, were assumed to be a plea such as the following: "My God, My God, why hast thou forsaken me?" "For some of those who stood by, when they heard it said, Behold, he calleth Elias." If those who stood by did not understand His words and were unable to give them the correct translation, but only guessed at their meaning, then those who recorded them later had no means of knowing their true significance. Again they interpreted what He said according to their own ideas, or according to what they would have spoken had they been in His place, without His great love and divine majesty.

The true interpretation of the words, "Eloi, Eloi, lama, sabachthani," is: "My God, My God, this is my destiny! For this was I sent!"

At the finish of His ordeal He cried with a loud

voice— and that voice was the triumphant cry of glory! "The Hosannas shout" of the soul! It was the exulting, triumphant shout of victory! And that cry was, "Father, into thy hands I commend my spirit!"

Only the divine Son of the Living God, our beloved, glorious Savior could have so completely glorified such a shameful experience and exalted so ignoble a death. The very world He came to save rejected Him. And only the Redeemer of the world could have transformed such a crowning indignity with honor and exalted it into eternal triumph and power and everlasting blessings for all who will only accept of His divine and holy offering—HIMSELF!

He shed His precious blood both in the garden and upon the cross to atone for our sins. He offered His sacred, pure, divine life of holy obedience and love for our sin-stained ones of darkness and rebellion and selfishness and pride. He willingly sacrificed His supreme, beautiful, perfect life that we could live. It was not only that we could have life, but have it "more abundantly—even life eternal!"

The gift Christ gave is redemption and the stupendous gift of vibrant, eternal life, here and now, if we will only accept of it. Through accepting of His offering we can be forgiven for our sins and transgressions and be given power to overcome our weaknesses and evils. By the power of His sacrifice and through the shedding of His precious blood we can follow the path He trod—and do the works which He did, namely "OVERCOME"—even "As he overcame." And as we overcome our weaknesses, which is the cause of our errors and evils and mistakes, we can become "purified, even as He is pure!" For such is the promise.

In such compassionate, divine assistance we need only have the courage to face our faults and then have the humility and the honesty to admit them, as we offer them to Him. Our very weaknesses are "The burden with which we are heavy laden." It is the burden of morality and its inherent, physical traits that is the almost unbearable load of each and every one. As we offer our weaknesses to Him, in a complete yielding, He is there to release us from them and to give us rest—along with the divine, stupendous power to overcome them forever. This is the divine "overcoming" that brings a complete fulfillment of every law and every divine accomplishment.

Praise be to God forever for an offering so gloriously powerful.

Christ freely gave the offering of Himself but each individual must willingly accept that sacrifice. It will never be forced upon a single soul. Freely was the gift given and freely must it be received. Not even the most fanatical, determined preachers have the power to force salvation or the glory of His divine redemption upon a single soul, though it has been tried.

And since Christ's offering was given freely it cannot be sold for money, though some have tried to collect for it also. His offering is held out to every humble, reaching, desiring individual of this polluted, tear-stained earth.

Such is the power and the love behind Christ's priceless gift of redemption, offered to a sinful, lost world—a world submerged in darkness. No individual has a monopoly upon His precious gift. And only those can be excluded who exclude themselves.

Yet there are those who still sell Him for a few pieces of silver as they preach about Him upon the Sabbath day then pass the contribution box to collect their reward—their pieces of silver—or their heaped up plates of greenbacks, claiming they are "worthy of their hire." These are they to whom He will say, "Depart from me ye accursed, I know ye not," for they have bypassed the "higher" way of attainment for a monetary price.

For those who do not accept of Christ's great offering of redemption and exaltation there still remains the salvaging experience known as "salvation." This is held out to those who through indifference, self-righteousness, unbelief, injustice, bigotry, or ignorance refuse His greater gift of perfect love, that they might "Overcome"—while in this life.

It is only in defiant wickedness and continued evil and the path of chosen rebellion and wanton sinning that one can lose permanently the gift Christ gave to the world. And even these must have so far advanced in understanding they knowingly reject His sacrifice and deliberately choose the darkness rather than the light.

Those, who, in humility and love seek to overcome, the ways of overcoming open wide. These noble ones do not need to be salvaged. They become exalted. And it is for each man to choose his own degree and his own eternal status of existence.

Christ's desire to redeem a world is just as intense now as it was that night in Gethsemane. His love is even more far reaching as He offers strength, wisdom, understanding and love to all who desire them. His infinite gifts of forgiveness, redemption and eternal life are still held out in divine, holy, wondrous loving power to all who desire to receive.

Christ gave Himself! All that is required of man is that he relinquish his weaknesses and his lusts and his selfishness and pride, which are the cause of his sins. And even in this ability to face himself and in the acknowledgement of his own imperfections man does not stand alone. Christ is always awaiting the invitation or the request to assist any and all who will only ask, for the promise is: "Ask and you shall receive!" And "Lo! I am with you always, even unto the end of the earth!"

In 1962 a new version of "The King of Kings" was portrayed upon the screen. And it was a dismal failure. Mary was given more power in that portrayal than her Son, the Redeemer of the world! He was pictured as a mere mortal while it was implied that she was divine. Let it be here known, Christ was not great because Mary was His mother. Rather was she great because He was her son.

The last scene of this powerless, uninspired movie showed Christ, the resurrected, risen Son of God, plodding up the hill from His tomb, clad in a dismal old gray shroud, without either power or light or glory! For shame! For shame to those who would belittle the magnitude of His glory and the deathless, triumphant power of His resurrection as He exalted His mortal body into eternal life, with the power to take it with Him.

None have lifted their eyes to behold His glory. Man has never comprehended the meaning of those wonderful words, *"Eyes single to the glory of God!"* How could man have possibly comprehended so great and powerful an invitation to behold and witness God's Almighty Glory, when Christ has been kept nailed to the cross down the centuries!

From the beginning the infant, "wrapped in swaddling clothes and lying in a manger," has been held out to the contemplation of man. Or the crucified Lord, nailed upon the cross, has been worshipped.

The cross has been the symbol of Christianity. And thus the two most impotent, helpless stages of Christ's mortal existence have been hallowed and acclaimed and placed eternally before the contemplative vision of man. Consequently none have lifted their eyes to behold the dynamic light and power of His glory and therefore none have been able to hold their eyes single to that glory. They have held their eyes single to the helpless, infant state of the new-born child and to the Savior nailed to the cross. And so it is that none look upward to behold His glory and none therefore have been able to begin to take upon themselves the reflection of that glory, that "They might become like Him!"

None have looked beyond the helpless, infant state to walk beside Him in His power as He trod upon the tumultuous Sea of Galilee. None have breathed in the wonder and the glory of His loving compassion as he healed the halt, the leperous, the afflicted and the blind. And so few have exulted in His dynamic words, "Lazarus, Come forth!"

Man in his blindness has insited upon worshipping the cross. And at one time almost depleted Europe with its crusades, carried under the banner of that cross.

Few have, even for a moment, lifted their eyes to behold Christ in His resurrected glory. If any individual had lifted his spiritual vision to behold the almost incomprehensible glory his eyes would have forever after been "single to that glory!" Any and all who will only lift their eyes to behold His divine, breathtaking glory will begin to take on that same glory.

When one is finally so "purified in his heart" and "cleansed from all sin" he can behold the face of Christ, he will see none of the tragic things which have been kept alive by those who have never understood the great wonder of His victorious, triumphant glory!

Only those two, impotent fractions of His life, portraying His most powerless states, are held out to the world as His life is remembered and contemplated. Never His glory!

Such promises as the following have been lost in the centuries of darkness: "And if your eye be single to my glory, your whole bodies shall be filled with light, and there shall be no darkness in you; and that body that is filled with light comprehendeth all things. Therefore, sanctify yourselves that your minds become single to God, and the days will come that you shall see him; for he will unveil his face unto you, and it shall be in his own time, and in his own way, and according to his own will!"

As one lifts the spiritual eyes of his understanding to behold the glory of Christ, and to contemplate His love and His victory, his eyes will become single to that glory. In lifting his vision above all mortal, earthbound ideas, he will be prepared to behold the face of Christ. And in the eyes of Jesus of Nazareth, exalted Son of the Living God, he will behold all the concentrated love of eternity and the understanding and compassion of the ages held in the complete forgiveness of God.

Such is the power and the glory and the tender love of the resurrected Messiah, the Savior of the world, the Son of the Living God! The great and mighty "King of Kings," the glory of the world! And those who behold Him will behold His glory, and forever after will their eyes be single to that glory and they too will begin to reflect it and to be filled with light.

And every soul who seeks diligently to KNOW HIM, not just to *know about him,* will eventually "behold His face, for He will unveil His face to them." Such is the eternal promise of heaven and such is your privilege to receive.

The sign of Christ's birth is the star. The sign of His crucifixion is the cross. But neither of these signs were meant to be worshipped. Only Christ Himself is worthy of our adoration and our love and praise!

Love Him! Adore Him! Worship Him! And let your eyes become single to His glory that you might be filled with the Light of It and with His love and with His power—forever and ever—

Amen.

WHAT IS VIBRATION?

Chapter V

Vibration is what an infant feels when cradled in the protective warmth of its mother's loving arms.

Vibration is what a child feels and responds to when its father tosses it gleefully into the air or its mother plays with it in gentle tenderness. It is quite possible that the parents might play a little too rough, even to the point of hurting the child, but as long as it is *play* the little one will laugh in joyous delight. However if the parents change their vibrations of love and pleasure and solicitous kindness, or lay a finger, ever so lightly, upon the little one in reproof or discord its little heart will break.

Vibrations sent out in wrath and anger can injure a child quite as much as physical punishment, especially if that child is sensitive.

Parents can literally "beat" their children into a state of unreasonable numbness, smoldering re-

WHAT IS VIBRATION?   63

bellion, open defiance, destructive hatred or into a
state of mental or physical retardment by their nagging, threatening vibrations and discords.

Children are especially sensitive to vibrations unless their spiritual reflexes have been dulled by a
continual shock treatment of negation and mis-treat-
ment. The vibrations with which a child is surrounded are more real to it than the walls of its
home and the tangible furnishings of the house in
which it dwells. The vibrations with which it is
surrounded are the real substance of its existence.
They are its life, whether pleasant or unpleasant.
And that child's entire life will be affected by the
discords of the ignorant, often selfish, moody adult
supervisors.

Vibration is also the exhilerating, ecstatic allness
of those in love. If these love vibrations were held
to and never allowed to diminish this world would
soon become a heaven. Married couples too often
forget their love for their mates as their love for
themselves is given predominance. Every accepted
offense is but the injured, little mortal-*self* feeling
sorry for *itself*. It is then the vibrations of hurt and
retaliation and resentment build up and increase
as they replace the vibrations of love and singing
happiness—and life becomes a long burden of painful endurance, retaliating actions, strident re-actions,
smoldering dislikes, nagging hate or lonely separation.

Vibration is the sound or tone that lingers in the
air long after the note has been struck upon a bell
or upon some musical instrument. Vibration is the

invisible manifestation of sound, or of thought, or of action. It is what remains after the visible cause has vanished.

Vibration is the lingering hurt of an unkind word. It is the fires of remorse, the essence of fear, the corrosive, degenerative, invisible, destructive potency of lust and dissipation. It is the undermining, disintegrating, hidden effects of hate. It is the consuming, revolting repulsiveness of greed. Vibration is the all-consuming fires of jealousy released in silence and in secret from an unloving, selfish heart to bring their own aftermath of destruction.

Vibration is the unseen, intangible world of cause and effect.

Vibration is light! It is also darkness, for all unseen forces are expressed in vibration. When active, the powers of both good and evil are manifest through the vibrating might of their rhythmed outpouring.

Light can only be made manifest through vibration. The light our eyes behold is vibration. By increasing the vibrations of joy and gladness and thanksgiving and loving praise the negative vibrations can be eliminated from one's life and the very element of "light will become subject" unto the individual. Light vibration is the penetrating, active energy of fulfilment for it opens the understanding and awakens the intellect to comprehend. It is the force that attunes one's entire being to the glory and the powers of heaven.

Positive vibrations of light and love always have

the efficacy to dispel and disperse the evil vibrations of negation and darkness when called upon to do so. This knowledge contains the method of using the laws of "righteousness" correctly. The positive vibrations of joy and happiness and expanding love have the power to completely dissipate every negative vibration of evil and dismay.

The positive, glorious vibrations of existence are the creative forces of life and light released into exuberating action and dynamic power. Life itself is a manifestation of vibration as one lays hold of its vibrant, tingling joy of being. And "Man is that he might have joy!" This is the purpose for which he was created. Within the exhilerating vibration of praise and love and gratitude is contained the singing wonder of the ever renewing life force, which can be increased and multiplied within anyone who will only use its powers and bring it forth from within himself. Within the holy essence of the exotic vibrations of joy and gladness and gratitude and praise is the very vibrancy of "THE LIFE MORE ABUNDANT!"

As one learns to control every vibration that goes out from him, as well as the vibrations that are hurled at him by another, he will grow into the sublime power of having the very force and essence of vibrant life increased within himself until the power of *life will become subject unto him.* Not only will such a one begin to manifest "The life more abundant" he will reach the point where "No one will be able to take his life from him—unless he

permits it," even as Christ expressed. Such a one
naturally becomes the master of life as it becomes
subject unto him. And in this glorious achievement
one receives also the gift of "LIFE ETERNAL!"

In having learned to control vibrations, as they
are released from within oneself or by another,
through the controlled power of thought, one can
actually become so filled with light he becomes
one with that Light. "Then there can be no darkness in him, and he will comprehend all things—
and God will unveil His face unto him."

The power of controlling one's vibrations, when
comprehended, is one of the most simple procedures
in existence. It is the road Christ traveled. It is the
road of power when one travels it knowingly. One's
dynamic powers of creation can be mis-used or
abused or they can be used with unlimited power
for good. One's vibrations can be weak, nil and
almost non-existent. Or they can be repulsive and
evil. Or they can contain the unspeakable powers
of heaven within their dynamic, creative release. It
is always up to the individual to select the caliber
of his released vibrations as he sends them out under
control. He can put all the energy of his heart, mind,
soul and strength into them and they will have the
power to sweep the earth and vibrate across the
universe. Or he can let his wandering, idle, unpro-
ductive, unprogressive thoughts absorb his potential
powers by exerting no control as his idle mind drifts
to and fro.

Those who desire to fulfill the laws of "righteousness" or who are determined to make the "right-use" of the divine forces which God has given to abide within must exert themselves if they would become powerful. They must begin to comprehend the inner workings of the creative laws of the universe—and of themselves. In taking hold of these inner forces it is quite possible and a very simple thing to be able to receive the fulfilling marvel of all the stupendous promises God has ever given to the children of men.

In seeking for this kingdom of power (within) one must truly begin to comprehend the stupendous energy released with every dynamic thought and feeling. As one begins to "hunger and thirst after righteousness" or for the might and the power to use the potential powers contained within himself, righteously, he will be prepared to step into a higher vibratory existence. He will then comprehend the limitless potentialities vested in himself—even the unspeakable powers of creation and of divinity— and "Of all that the Father has."

Every caliber of thought has its own vibrations. Every word, every emotion contains dynamic potency and must of its own nature release the vibrations which pertain to it. No one can think, or feel, or speak without sending out the vibrations he creates with his released thoughts and words and feelings and actions. These vibrations he releases are his own creations. And he will be judged by them if they are worthless and idle. He will be destroyed by them if they are strident and evil. He will be forever glorified and exalted by them if he has been the master and brought them into subjection.

As one begins to use the laws of that which leads to all "righteousness" he will find that it is truly the kingdom within which contains all the laws of heaven and the powers thereof. These immeasurable, dynamic forces of stupendous power are man's to master and to control in majesty and eternal, ever-lasting, unspeakable glory. Or they are his to release in uncontrolled violence to wreak their havoc upon himself, his loved-ones perhaps, or his associates or upon the world. And he himself will be held account-able.

Vibration is also the manifestation of Spirit—and when contacted and released with understanding it is the very power of God in action as it flows forth from the individual in breathtaking waves of light. Vibration is always active. Vibrations are released and sent out by the thought forces of those who re-lease them. Vibrations are the very force of creative power, used for good or ill, according to the devel-opment and understanding, or lack of it, of him who releases them. Vibrations are released with every thought and feeling whether their creator is aware of what he is doing or not. Yes, "All that the Father has is yours!" And the stirring command to: "LET THERE BE—LIGHT" or love, or peace, or joy, or happiness, or plenty, according to the individual's need is within his power to bring forth. And "IT IS SO!" Or, "IT WAS GOOD!"

In comprehending the unspeakable power contained within the vibrations of one's own creating, man can indeed bring all things under his feet or under his control. Such a one has the power to bring all things into harmony and beauty so that the inner glory of God's Kingdom, of which he himself is a part, can be brought forth into the outer realm of his existence. And thus can all things become subjected unto him, in love and beauty and perfection.

As one learns to control his own thoughts and actions and re-actions, permitting no negative, vile, craven, lust-filled, evil, hate-filled thought or feeling to be generated or released through him, he will become powerful. "And all things will become subject unto him, both in heaven and on earth the Light and the Life; the Spirit and the Power, sent forth by the will of the Father, through Jesus Christ, His Son."

These almost incomprehensible powers are spiritual, nevertheless they can be released, directed and commanded by those who will fulfill the highest laws of their own beings. These released vibrations are the cause and the effect of every condition upon this earth, whether national, or individual, or whether the whole wide world is included.

The vibrations which are sent out with every word, emotion, action and reaction are the creations of man and are eternally his own. They will bless or condemn him. They will exalt mankind or help to destroy it. It is for each individual to decide the full measure of his creative powers—for good or ill. If one's released vibrations are only selfish, lust-filled and evil then that individual will more speedily be destroyed by the forces of darkness he releases through his own being.

As individuals learn of the unspeakable, stupendous power of the vibrations they release, and learn to control them, their lives will be straightened out and become enhanced in beauty and glorified in power. And as individuals bring the vibrations they release under control, or into subjection, the world itself will be benefitted until the evils of this earth can be healed—and its tears dried.

"The leaves from the Tree of Life, which are to be used for the healing of the nations," are the released, living vibrations which man himself must begin to comprehend and use according to the laws of righteousness.

When these vibrations are comprehended and used, even by a few, the world will more swiftly be prepared to step into a new phase of existence.

As one learns to comprehend the full power of the vibrations he releases in his everyday living and exalts himself into the full majesty of their controlling he will be able to use the very powers of eternity.

As one lets only vibrations of love and joy and gratitude and happiness be released from within himself, in a singing glory of eternal, vibrant power, he will KNOW the truth of every promise Christ ever gave to the world and he will be able also to "do the works which Christ did—even greater works."

As an individual learns to overcome his own vibrations of wrath, anger, hate, greed, lust, and selfishness, he will have the superb power "to completely overcome the evils of his life." Even the destructive vibrations of worry, which are but the released vibrations of his own fear thoughts, can be eliminated instantly by the exalting vibrations of increased love, or love for God, sent out in a vibration of praising glory. And it must always be remembered, "love casts out all fear."

With the first glimmer of understanding of these inherent powers, contained right within oneself, it is possible to begin immediately to use one's own released vibrations of love and peace to quiet discords between friends, members of one's own family, acquaintances or strangers. This is not accomplished through words. It is done by "POWER." "For my kingdom is not in *word* but in *power*." This ability to establish peace, even in wrangling assemblies, is accomplished as one silently exerts his thoughts to send out vibrant, powerful waves of love and peace and quiet. This power can be used at all times. It increases with use.

To comprehend the power of vibrations, which are created and generated by the force of one's own thought actions, one can truly develop the dynamic power of bringing all things and all conditions into subjection. These are the very powers of heaven, which man can take hold of and use as "all things become subject unto him, both in heaven and on earth."

Again, you may gasp and say, "Blasphemy!" And again the challenge stands forth, "Prove all things!"

No greater truths than these have ever before been written. These are "The great and mavelous things which God has kept hidden up from the foundation of the world because of the gross wickedness of unbelief."

And at last, I have been instructed to write these "Great, heretofore, unspeakable truths," for such was the promise of Almighty God unto the children of men. And the time is at hand.

These are the gifts and powers Christ held out for me to view when He came that night to heal lovely Linda, which account has been described in the book, "Ye Are Gods." Christ's arms were laden with the breathtaking gifts of life and of eternity. And with infinite love He explained, "I am so anxious and eager to bestow my choice gifts upon men as soon as they are prepared to receive them!" And I beheld those gifts and marveled. They contained the glory of health and happiness, of wisdom and understanding and the limitless power of plenty and abundance. There was the power not only to rule over every condition upon the earth, but the power to reach out into eternity and leave one's imprint upon the very stars.

This is the record of His divine laws being placed in your hands for fulfilment. Guard these truths well and rejoice in their glory of unspeakable worth as they become your own to use and to enjoy and to fulfill in eternal, triumphant glory.

Control your worthy vibrations and the evil ones will automatically be overcome. Exhilarate that vibrant life force of love and praise and gratitude and receive "the life more abundant!" Rejoice and give thanks for such dynamic, almost unspeakable powers which God has vested in you! Be increasingly aware of them and use them with all your God-given intelligence—and become powerful.

The way is yours—and the powers also. Use them for you are the instrument through which these celestial vibrations of power and glory must be released. And you are the musician, or the creator of these vibrations. And the melody or the discord is your own.

There are those who are almost vibrationless. These are the ones who never feel intensely or think dynamically. For these it is a more simple thing to begin to control vibrations. Vibrations, for them, will automatically come under control as they develop more intensified thinking and feeling habits.

Those who are already dynamic, who have lived and thought with deep intensity, the need to keep a continual guard around themselves for a period of time, as they set out upon this pathway of power, will be quite necessary. For them the problem is to bring into control every powerful, intense, dynamic vibration so that these concentrated, vigorous energies might be brought into complete subjection. In the controlling of vibrations the individual soon becomes the master and is no longer tossed to and fro by the storms and tempests of life.

To have these stupendous powers of creation brought into control the individual must comprehend the laws of their "right use" or righteousness. He must guard himself against every feeling of lack and inadequacy, against every disturbing thought or word or act. He, with this power and understanding, can, like Christ, exalt any condition of adversity into triumphant achievement.

In the commencement of one's journey into these higher powers of achievement he must be doubly cautious at first, for he will become supersensitive. Evil, loud, discordant vibrations can become shattering as they rise up to resist his control and his authority. Unless one is understanding and determined the trait of "flying off the handle" will be intensified.

But for the strong, dynamic, determined ones the path of overcoming becomes so breathtakingly intriguing and so filled with power he soon becomes the master. He quickly proves that this is the pathway of unlimited power as he learns to bring all things under control. "And all things become subjected unto him, both in heaven and on earth, the life and the light; the Spirit and the power, sent forth by the will of the Father, through Jesus Christ, His Son."

Such is the promise! And such is the power of learning to control or bring into subjection those vibrations one automatically releases under pressure and stress—or under the moments of deep contemplation and exalted thinking.

It is quite necessary that one travel this path in humility and prayer as he sings forever the "New Song" out of the joy of his own heart.

To control vibrations until they are brought into complete subjection one must not only learn to control his thoughts, but his *feelings!* It is in one's thinking that vibrations are sired and in one's emotions that they are released or delivered.

"It isn't what goes into a man that defiles him, but what comes out of him." It is his released vibrations that either glorify and exalt him or defile and destroy him.

THE PATH OF POWER

Chapter VI

The Celestial Song of Creation, the ecstatic vibration of praise and love and gratitude, which is the released Light of Christ, will exalt any individual and lift him above his present status of existence, regardless of what it may be. One has only to lay hold of that vibration of singing, triumphant glory with a constant awareness as he releases the creative powers of heaven and "uses them rightly." The releasing of these higher vibrations can never fail to sustain and exalt one into a state of higher enlightenment in an ever continual path of advancement.

These higher vibrations, which man can release, are a spiritual reality which have the power to gather together into tangible form the elements that are "unseen." This ethereal "substance of things hoped for" can be solidified and made tangible as one uses the power of faith, united with the vibrations of Christ's holy Light. "The substance of things hoped for" is brought forth into the material world of concrete reality or into visible form just by applying the laws which govern it. As the laws are applied both the laws and powers become subject unto the one who uses them rightly—or "righteously." The breathtaking power of the law, when released in praise and love and gratitude, not only exalts one but fulfills the needs of him who will only apply it with exalted understanding.

As one keeps an awareness of the sacred, wondrous vibrations of singing glory alive within his being, in a constant splendor of rejoicing devotion, the condition in which he lives will be changed into one of exalting progress and happiness and increased understanding and power.

As one proves the truth of this vibrant Song of ecstasy, which is but the releasing of Christ's divine Light within himself, the power becomes his own to use.

One has only to live any of the divine laws Christ gave in order to prove them. And when one lives the higher laws, or keeps the commandments, then is "God bound." The promises must be fulfilled when the laws are fulfilled. The laws are irrevocable and the promises sure. They cannot be changed nor set aside. They are eternal. They are unfailing. They are perfect and powerful.

As one *masters* that Celestial Song of Creation, or that glorious "New Song, which none but the righteous can learn," he becomes a master. And it is then that the very powers of heaven are released into his life.

Such a one can no longer be either mediocre, a failure or remain mere mortal. His very application of the laws of unutterable power, as he releases the vibrations right within himself, bestow upon him the complete understanding of how to climb the glorious, lighted highway of exaltation in an ever increasing melody of rejoicing as his own potentialities are developed and brought forth.

This exquisite song becomes not only a singing glory in one's soul, it becomes a tangible, breathtaking power in his life as he is continually lifted into an ever higher status of development. This is the "growing from grace to grace," or the advancing continually from one degree of enlightened progress into another. This is the dynamic method of spiritual growth which Christ used. In the application of this wondrous power of divine advancement one is continually lifted from one level of progress into an ever higher level.

These vibrations of praise and love and gratitude, when released from a human heart, are "The New Song." This is also the method by which one releases the eternal Light of Christ, and It thereafter becomes subjected unto that individual. It is truly the divine vibration of exalting Light in which one becomes completely clothed as he learns to hold himself within its exotic glory of enfoldment. Each individual must progress by his own desiring and efforts to the point where he can clothe himself in this holy apparel of light if he wishes to fulfill the law of his own being. Or as the inspired writer of the "Odes of Solomon" testified: "And I CLOTHED MYSELF IN LIGHT and acquired a body free from sorrow or affliction or pain."

This powerful vibration of light is beyond the mere mind of mortal man to fully comprehend simply because man has never lifted his eyes to behold the glory of God, nor kept them single to that glory. Neither has he learned to vibrate in the exuberating excellence of God's Almighty power.

As one lays hold of the vibrations of praise and love and gratitude he overcomes all the darkness and negation and evils of his life. The follies and the fears, the weaknesses and doubts are banished as he is given the power of complete mastery over every cell and tissue and fibre of his body. As he gains this control every atom vibrates in an harmonious rhythm of perfect peace. The warring elements and tissues respond and the lion lays down with the lamb.

This "New Song" is not only released from one's mind and heart, it is released from his entire being in a glory that is impossible to describe to those who have not yet experienced it. This is not a song of words, but of power. And it is true, "that none but the righteous can learn it."

As one masters this divine symphony of celestial harmony he will have brought forth that divine Light of Christ right within himself and henceforth *"that light will be subject unto him."* And as he learns to use that Light the very gift of life will become his to command and to bring forth in its radiant splendor of abundance, so that he need never die.

Clothed in this holy vibration of Light, or singing praise and love and gratitude, one could descend into the very depths of Hell and Hell would be transformed. It would have to open wide its barred, sealed doors for it could not possibly contain the fulness of that divine, holy Light.

This is the released Light Christ used in His descent into Hell. If He had carried any resentment with Him, or if He had mentally resisted His crucifixion or held any blame or condemnation out toward His accusers or self-pity for Himself He could not have achieved so great an assignment.

As Christ entered the closed confines of Hell with His great Light of love and praise and glorious, singing gratitude, the one-way gates of Hades had to open wide and the prisoners were released. And to them Christ gave the laws of their own advancement from the very depths of darkness and failure and despair. It was even as Peter so beautifully revealed in his record: "For Christ hath once suffered for sins, the just for the unjust, that he might bring us to God, being put to death in the flesh, but quickened by the spirit: by which also he went and preached unto the spirits in prison; which formerly were disobedient, when once the long-suffering of God waited in the days of Noah." (I Peter 3:18-20).

The days of Noah had been over fifteen centuries before the divine ministry of Christ upon the earth, climaxed by His descent into Hell, to set the prisoners free. Such was Christ's power! And such was the use He made of it in every condition and upon every occasion.

No resentments, no demoralizing self-pity, no cloying dislikes were upon Him. In the pure, holy vibration of exulting praise and perfect love and divine gratitude and forgiveness He entered those realms clothed in the vibrations of eternal glory and the very doors of Hell had to open.

Any man can use these same keys or vibrations to open up the doors to any hellish, impossible condition on this earth. He can rise above every anguished sorrow, every gloomy, depressing, devastating situation or heart-breaking condition by clothing himself in the vibrations of Light, simply by constant love and praise and gratitude.

As one learns to release those glorious vibrations of power he can literally clothe himself in Light and it will prove to be the "sacred armour of Christ," against which no evil force in existence can have any power. No adverse condition can possibly continue to exist under God's eternal plan of perfect control as man uses those powers aright. And all things become *possible* to him who uses these dynamic, unspeakable powers "righteously." This is how the powers of heaven are brought forth into their true perfection of everlasting, superb release and divine use.

One can so completely clothe himself in this divine, holy vibration of Light no evils can touch him, no dismays come near him or darkness thwart his progress.

As One travels this glorious road of rejoicing, singing, vibrating glory, releasing the powers of triumphant overcoming, he is traveling the road of sonship, even to the completion of his own fulfilment and divinity. This is the Path of ever-increasing, glorious, sublime power as man takes hold of the wonder of his own perfecting.

The glory of praise and love and gratitude, when released from a human heart, *is* Light. As this Light is increased until it fills every cell and fibre and tissue of one's being one becomes literally filled with Light, so that he not only comprehends all things, *"The Light becomes subject unto him!"* He can command it! He will be able to use its limitless, unspeakable powers to accomplish those things which before seemed to be impossible. And as each cell and atom of his being is embued with this Light he will never die! "Believest thou this?"

It is the mastery of that divine, glorious "New Song" that brings the Light and the Life into subjection to the individual who learns to release it in a constant symphony of beauty from the depths of his own being. And henceforth that one will have the power to command that "Light to stand forth" as he uses it according to the dynamic needs at hand. Or as Christ said, "He will be able to do all things which are expedient unto me." And those "ex-

pedient" things are the things that arise as one
journeys over the earth in a directed service of love
and obedience.

As that gift of Light becomes subjected unto an
individual he will also be given the power to bring
forth the pure radiance of that Light to heal and
bless and to restore. And in doing so he will receive
"The Life more abundant" for it too will become
subjected unto him.

Praise and give thanks without ceasing for "He
who is thankful in all things will be made glorious,
and the things of this earth will be added unto him,
a hundred-fold; yea, more!" In this higher vibration of existence one will truly be "filled with Light
and comprehend all things!" And "all things will
become subject unto him, both in heaven and on
earth; the Light and the Life; the Spirit and the
power!" This is the point of power God covets for
all. These are the gifts Christ holds out, waiting for
man to prepare himself to receive. These powers
and gifts are the real meaning of life itself. This is
the point of progress in which one begins to take
on immortality, "or to evolve from the man kingdom into the God Kingdom."

Then it will be that all things are provided from
the universal supply, or from the living atoms, *waiting to become.*" And, as stated in one of the preced-
ing books, "an atom is a ray of radiant light curled
upon itself." This knowledge is profound, even as
the knowledge of the atom itself is the greatest mystery of all mysteries. If one can fully comprehend

an atom he will comprehend the universe and the laws of creation. Within the atom is contained the fulness of all things.

And God has given man the power, when he is prepared to use it correctly, to bring the light into subjection. By this law, or power, man will be able to command those rays of radiant light to curl upon themselves to form atoms, and to gather them in sufficient quantities to supply all his needs. This substance of atoms, "waiting to become" *is faith* as man begins to use it. This ethereal substance becomes real as the spiritual material becomes manifest in tangible form.

These elements or atoms or rays of radiant light that have not yet curled upon themselves, are "waiting to become." They must obey the law of their existence when he, with authority, or with a belief strong enough to command them, puts forth the command for them to fulfill the pattern or desire his mind holds forth.

There is no such thing as empty space or a vacuum in nature. The entire universe is filled with cosmic rays along with those vibrant, living rays of radiant light rushing forth to meet their destiny. There are countless "zillions" of these minute, radiant light rays in space. And there are a thousand times a billion trillion quadrillion countless "zillions" being created and sent forth every instant of every day, for when God said, "Let there be Light" He started upon their journey of existence everything that could possibly "become" in time and in eternity. This is creation. And it is going on constantly.

These infinite, tiny little rays of radiant light are the "substance of things hoped for." They are endowed with spirit and intelligence and life and unspeakable power. They were neither created nor made. They were moved upon by the command and the Will of God and are thus quickened and sent forth to fulfill His dynamic plan of creation. And these rays will obey the impelling command of him who has perfected himself and learned to exercise the principle of faith, which is, "the substance of things hoped for," or the spiritual material or element out of which all things are formed.

Man has failed completely to comprehend the resources awaiting his command as he purifies himself to the degree in which he can be entrusted with their limitless wealth and abundance. Man has so set his heart and mind upon gaining the treasures of this world to appease his insatiable greeds and lusts and selfishness he has never realized that those "boundless treasures of heaven" are right at his fingertips. These are the treasures that cannot be stolen, or destroyed, or contaminated. There is sufficient to give every man, woman and child everything they can possibly need or use or desire. It is not even necessary to struggle or slave for them, or to rob from others, or to steal or murder.

In order to gain access to this boundless, unlimited treasure-house of abundance one needs only to work upon himself as he develops his own potentialities into their full perfection. Then it will be that "all things will be added unto him" for he "will comprehend all things" and "all things will become subject unto him."

In this advanced state one will be given the power to bring forth from the divine, universal, unending supply of Almighty God, all that he needs or could ask for or desire. And with this power he will never need to cheat or rob another or to hoard up chests and banks full of wealth wherein "moth and rust can corrupt and thieves break through and steal."

These treasures and powers of creation are still waiting the exploration of those who are willing to put Christ's teachings fully to the test. The laws of these dynamic powers are all contained within His exalting laws of glorified obedience. None have "believed" enough to live the laws which govern this boundless, breathtaking fulfillment.

The developed ability, within man, to give praise and love and gratitude will purify one more speedily than any other vibration possible to release as it prepares one to take hold of the creative laws of the universe. The perfected force of this divine Christ vibration of love and praise and thanksgiving must be obeyed and the very rays of radiant, spiritual light can be commanded to form themselves into atoms. And those atoms can be directed to gather and coagulate into tangible substance. These divine rays of radiant light, of which the boundless space of the entire universe is filled, will form themselves into the more material form of atoms, which, in turn, will gather together into any substance that can be "hoped for" or desired.

The law is: as one holds to his desires unwaveringly and continually gives thanks for whatever it is he is asking, "and does not doubt in his heart, he shall have whatsoever he asks."

Thus can "the light become subject unto man" as he purifies himself and opens up his heart and mind to "believe," and lifts his vision until it "becomes single to the glory of God." As one fulfills the laws of "righteousness" he will automatically become "filled with light and comprehend all things." And "All things will become subject unto him, both in heaven and on earth; the light and the life; the spirit and the power, sent forth by the will of the Father, through Jesus Christ, His Son."

These are the powers and the keys of creation and of dominion and of glory. This is the return to the Edenic estate when one "no longer needs to labor for the things that perish" nor needs to "till the ground by the sweat of his brow" in order to supply his livelihood. In this condition one no longer remains in this "lone and dreary world." It is transformed before him—and for him.

So are the promises and the blessings awaiting those who "overcome."

When one develops the power to comprehend the Light and to bring it forth it will henceforth be subject unto him. He will assuredly reach the point where he will "comprehend all things" as a normal youth will mature into manhood. "And God will unveil his face to him . . . Remember this great and last promise. Cast away your idle thoughts and your EXCESS of laughter far from you."

This divine song of singing, joyous ecstasy is not a "slap-happy," irresponsible condition of uncontrolled hilarity. It is not an hilarious condition at all. Rather is this great, glorious, ecstatic song of praising glory the state of perfect control of mind and body and soul for it is the power of God in dynamic action.

"Nothing is impossible to him who believes," or who will *be* and *live* according to the laws of the higher Kingdom, the Kingdom of heaven, or the Kingdom of his soul. This glorious Kingdom is a Kingdom of Light and love and power and understanding and of increased, exalting vibrations of eternal creation. It is the Kingdom of joyous ecstasy and of love and ever increasing glory—"and few there be who find it." Yet it is always awaiting those who will only fulfill the laws pertaining to it. Yes! "Live the laws and you will *know!*"

HOW DIVINE POWER IS VESTED IN MAN

Chapter VII

Spiritual powers can only be safely entrusted to those who have grown into their use by proper degrees as they master the laws which govern them. The great powers of heaven must be earned by one's living the higher laws until those laws become a very part of his being. He must reach the point where nothing can influence him to use them amiss, as Moses did in bringing forth water from the stone, then taking credit unto himself. One must first reach the point where his eyes are truly "single to the glory of God." This is not an idle phrase. It is a condition those must reach who desire to be entrusted with power.

There have been and are those who are so desirous of being chosen and endowed with power before they have grown into the measure of their own development they would rend it from the very throne of God. And such, though their intentions are of the best, would perhaps destroy themselves. These impatient ones, desirous of proving their own greatness, go rushing out to take hold of anyone and everyone whom they assume has any power. They work on the patience of others instead of upon themselves. These misguided ones are totally unprepared to use the powers of heaven rightly even if they were thus endowed. The powers of heaven can only be handled by those who, through the overcoming of themselves and the perfecting of love, are prepared to use them correctly or "righteously."

They are like children demanding a thunderbolt to play with.

And there are those misguided ones, or over-ambitious individuals who are concentrating their efforts on trying to flag down a flying saucer, instead of working upon themselves. Anyone who is prepared will be acknowledged and given his assignment of service. And the first assignment for every individual is to prepare himself. The futile efforts to take hold of that which is not yet earned only proves their unworthiness and unpreparedness.

These blessed, misinformed, misguided individuals must be brought to realize that no such outward strivings and clamorous demands are of any help, but only retard their progress to true attainment. This demand for power that one might awe the minds of men as he stands upon the pinnacle of the temple is but a human trait. But such human traits and cravings for show and acknowledgement must be overcome as one evolves from the man, or human, kingdom into the divine kingdom. And there are no shortcuts. Only by constant prayer and true humility can the path of perfection be trod.

The following chapter contains the first laws of true service. They are pure and beautiful and exquisitely divine. And every aspiring individual who is truly seeking for "righteousness" can use them from now on to heal and bless and to help restore.

The "hungering and thirsting after righteousness" is always the first step of attainment. This hungering and thirsting opens the whole soul wide to receive. The physical seals are gradually removed and his spiritual faculties are awakened to true service. As the seal is removed from the heart it too is opened in a melting, humble tenderness as the love of God begins to be poured forth through the center of his being with an increasing power to bless and to love and so to heal and to renew.

held and to receive the appeasement of his hunger

One, whose soul is thus opened wide to compre- and his thirst, will be prepared to begin to comprehend the great TRUTH and the law which governs it. He will be rewarded by the attunement of his whole soul being opened to hear the voice and the minute, individual instructions of God—for God will become his instructor.

In this holy process of growth one learns to "listen and to *be still*." His moments of intense, high devotion increase in frequency and duration. This "listening" is not done with one's physical ears but with the spiritual ears as one begins to receive his answers and his instructions through the ears of his soul and direct from God, instead of from man. This will be the only method of instruction in the years to come "for they will need no man to teach them, for God Himself will be their teacher." And none of His instructions nor His wisdom nor His knowledge is foolishness nor wasted. Any who prepare themselves to be taught of God will advance into the powers of eternity speedily and surely.

This method of inner instruction is the only method that cannot be duplicated, contaminated nor bring deception with it. This inner method of receiving knowledge, as one hungers and thirsts, is the only one that can fulfill the laws of righteousness as one searches for His Kingdom and its eternal truths.

Righteousness is something that cannot be put on from without, like a mantle or a robe. Righteousness must be brought forth from within. Neither can it be found on the outside. Nor can it be borrowed nor taken from another. Righteousness is a degree of development that one grows into by deep devotion, pure humility and constant prayer. It is reached by a constant searching or hungering and thirsting of the mind and heart to know and serve God, and God only.

As one places himself in tune with God he learns the deeper lessons of eternity. He begins to comprehend that the "learning of the world is indeed foolishness to the Lord." It is as one's whole soul seeks to *know* TRUTH and the will of God that the appeasement of his inward hungering and thirsting begins to find a holy satisfaction as he feasts with the Lord.

One of the essential requisites to be prepared to receive this inner instruction is the cultivation and development of that glorious, beautiful, divine gift of humility. This gift is most stupendously exquisite as it is brought forth in the full unfolding of its breathtaking glory. No gift so clothes an individual in shining radiance except, of course, the fully developed Christ Light as it is brought forth in its fulness.

And this gift of humility is perhaps the most elusive of all virtues because it cannot be seen by mortal eyes. And it can so often be duplicated or counterfeited by a sham, even groveling meekness that is completely repellent when comprehended. Humility is a splendor of the soul that is developed by an adoration of God and a love so complete it opens the deep, inner core of one's being to the divine Will of God in an utter surrender. In this love the proud, pompous, vain, little mortal-self, that is always reaching for credits and rewards and attention, is lifted up and exalted into the true, divine self in which no boasting is necessary, nor indeed is it permissible.

Personal pride and the little mortal-self must be left behind before one can possibly be entrusted with the divine powers of heaven. It is as one grows humble and learns to "listen" in true reverence that he begins to move forward into the rhythmed wonder of his own spiritual growth. And it is in this inward growth that the mortal weaknesses are outgrown and eliminated.

When Reason and I had been married for a year, and had had no time in which to enjoy or even get acquainted, we had our first vacation. We spent it down in the Pennsylvania hills in fasting and prayer. At the end of the first week I beheld, written in flame, over my head these words: "Dear Lord, give us eyes single to thy glory, WITH THE GIFT OF HUMILITY! Let every thought be in control and every word be for your honor!"

It was out beyond our reach, but in hungering and desiring to fulfill it came a continual unfolding of the will of God. And only now have I been permitted to share this sacred experience with those of you who wish to fulfill all righteousness.

When the impelling splendor of loving humility is attained then can the great, everlasting powers of Almighty God begin to be placed in one's hands. And only then will one be truly prepared to possess such powers, otherwise he could not possibly use the laws of righteousness righteously. It is only in love and deep reverence that such unspeakable powers can be placed within the grasp of those who are still in mortality. One must have begun "to evolve from the man kingdom into the God Kingdom" as his soul grows and develops according to the degree of the "hungering and the thirsting" that he has developed. The law of God is that anyone who truly "hungers and thirsts after righteousness" must be fed or filled. And this food is a spiritual food "That the world knows not of." And the drink is the out-flowing Spirit of Almighty God as it is shed forth through the hearts of the children of men.

When the divine powers of heaven are entrusted, even in a lesser degree, to any person who is not purified and cleansed from all sin he will begin to use them unrighteously in most instances. He will undertake his work in all righteousness and without realizing it he begins to work in self-righteousness as he assumes that he cannot possibly err. He begins to believe that no matter what he does it is correct and that he has the power to sway heaven and that it will obey his voice. Thus, without realizing it, he may begin to use his knowledge to take away the free-agency of his fellowmen, to bring them under his control, to issue unworthy decrees and unrighteous dominion. He may not even be aware that he is seeking to use the authority of God unworthily as he seeks to block the door of heaven to those who would enter. In his blindness he may even become a dictator who has no esteem nor feelings for the rights of others. Such will soon begin to use under-handed, "gestapo" methods to justify his actions or to prove his infalibility. He will subtly begin to bear false witness to humiliate and disprove the integrity of those who resist his decrees. And before he is aware of it he is no longer one divinely chosen. He actually begins to fight against God instead of to serve him. The very heavens weep over such who have corrupted the very term and meaning of "righteousness" to glorify their evil, selfish, self-righteousness. They have become fallen angels and realize it not.

In such the human weaknesses will become continually more manifest than the sacred powers of heaven as such a one seeks to use the divine powers for self-glory and for show as he begins to take credit and honors to himself.

This is the natural law of the flesh and he who has not overcome the flesh will fulfill the mortal law of his own vanity and pride as his physical desire for acclaim takes over.

To be entrusted with divine, holy powers, while still subject to human weaknesses, is dangerous beyond ordinary man's comprehension. One must have stepped out beyond the measure of his own personal desires if he will fulfill the full measure of his own glorious possibilities and use the divine powers and gifts of God righteously.

Only those who have, in a measure, earned such rights of power are given them, even in a minor degree, lest they do untold damage and eventually destroy themselves—and others.

Even those who have earned the right to authority, perhaps before ever they came to earth, are very apt to lose it through misuse. These special ones usually come with an inner knowing of importance and wishing to impress others with that importance they begin to use the powers of God unrighteously in order to put across the little mortal-self. In their search for approval and honors and worldly acclaim they relinquish their right to the honors and powers of heaven.

This unholy desecration and misuse of the divine powers of God is *Black Magic!* And within it is contained all the evils of darkness and mystery and deceits.

Such a man was Hitler.

And there are many more. Such, in their pride, begin to yearn so ardently for powers and attention they have not yet been fully endowed with they will make such a great show and a startling pretense to the authority of heaven they may, "if possible, deceive the very elect." If such arrogant ones are challenged or rebuked, or even gently warned, they will receive no criticism. To them it is God who has erred and with all their rebellion exercised they make it their duty to set Him aright, along with His whole heavenly kingdom and its divine laws.

There are those today, in high places, who are dangerous men. And though some of them believe they are serving God in their proud, self-righteousness they are unjust in their dealings, deficient in their wisdom, lacking in humility and are committing great evils. They are dangerous both to themselves and to the world as they use their power, and their authority to put across themselves and their opinions and beliefs. Such seek ever to gain the hearts of men, even as they subtlely blind the eyes of their followers to truth. They ignore the everlasting

decree that: "God will not be mocked!" Nor will
He sanction the selfish, unrighteous use of any of
His laws or powers for selfish adulation or personal
glory. Those who seek to use His divine powers unrighteously, in any degree whatsoever, will soon be
left unto themselves, bleak and desolate and forsaken
and utterly rejected.

So do not be impatient if the holy powers, you
so earnestly desire, are not yet placed in your hands.
It is only for your own protection and your own
safety that they are still withheld.

But you may be sure, oh noble aspirant for truth
and for righteousness, that the powers will be placed
in your possession as soon as you have proved yourself ready for the responsibility they entail. Such
holy, almost unspeakable authority of might and
power is entirely too sacred and too dynamic to be
flaunted before the eyes of men to awe their minds
with YOU.

Remember, that from the moment these dynamic
powers are entrusted to you you will be held doubly
accountable, before God, for your every thought and
word and act and for your every released vibration.
Whereas now, you are only held accountable for
your intentions.

If you are still desirous of receiving the divine
powers of God *that you might use them for the good
of man* then begin to pray for those who despitefully
use you and persecute you. This is a way in which
the good you accomplish can be immeasurable.

Such good is done without ostentation or fan-fare.

It is done silently, and in secret. "And the Father, who seeth in secret shall reward you openly." In this use of God's power there is no way to tempt one to boast of his accomplishments, for only heaven knows of the infinite, wonderful good that such a method can achieve. This is power which cannot be used to be seen of men. And as one uses this silent method of love and blessing he is growing into his own stature of fulfilment.

This subtle, inner obedience of out-pouring love, as one prays for his enemies, is the beginning of the works which Christ Himself did. The first works must be accomplished through the fullest obedience to the sacred laws of "righteousness" or "right-use-ness." These sacred laws of the Kingdom, which is within, are the inner laws of a man's own being that can not lay claim to awards and honors and credits. To fulfill these divine, inner laws truly and honorably and lovingly, for love will automatically develop their intensity and power, speedily prepares one to accomplish the "works which Christ accomplished."

In the fulfilling of this sacred, divine, power of praying for your enemies will give you the power of forgiveness. And in your forgiving you will be forgiven for all your mistakes, errors and transgressions so that you will not need to drag them along to hold you back from your own divine fulfilment.

Pray and bless and give thanks continually, without ceasing.

Pray for the pure privilege of praying! Pray! Pray

for those you love and especially for those whom you have hated—and for those who have, or do, hate you! Pray out of the fulness of your heart and love will begin to flow out through you to help heal and bless a world. Pray always and you will grow into a dynamic person as you learn to "walk with God." In doing this you will be fulfilling one of the earliest laws given to man: "Do all that you do in the name of the Lord; and call upon the name of the Son forevermore!"

And as you pray let your heart be opened wide to appreciate the privilege and power of prayer. Let this gift of appreciation grow and expand as it reaches out to enfold your surroundings and your every gift of abundance.

Thank God for every minute blessing. Thank Him for your daily bread. Thank Him for your physical blessings, though they may not be perfect at the present time. Continue to thank Him for the degree of health you do have and that spark of life will expand and increase until you are endowed with the "Life more abundant!"

Never take any blessing for granted. "For he who is thankful in all things will be made glorious! And the things of this earth will be added unto him a hundred-fold; Yea, more!" Remember, the law of gratitude is the spiritual law of increase and multiplication. If you have but three loaves of bread and two small fishes and no more food in sight or any way of earning more, then bless and give thanks

and watch that small supply multiply to fulfill your
needs.

In loving silence pray the Lord's prayer, often.
And, if you are in need or in doubt as to where
your daily bread is coming from, stress the words
in love and gratitude as you lovingly repeat the
phrase, "Give us this day our daily bread."

As you bless and give thanks continually, for every
blessing, asking God to supply your daily bread,
the gifts and power of increase, and finally of divine creation will be placed in your hands. These
are sacred keys. They are powerful keys, which man
has ignored as he has struggled along his mortal
road seeking ever to "earn his bread by the sweat
of his brow." And often, when his sweat has worn
out or dried up, he has stood bleak and hungry, even
while the keys of plenty and of abundance were
right in his hand.

Any man from his hovel of the past could be
placed in one of the modern mansions of today,
and unknowingly live in ignorance and in darkness,
unless he understood the simple method of turning
a tiny switch, perhaps concealed within the wall.

Man has brought forth many magical things. But
the great and dynamic powers of eternity have been
just beyond his comprehension. They have never
been beyond his reach. They have always been right
at hand, and the method of using them. But man
has not believed in the magic wonder of God's power
to fulfill every word and every promise, so he has
ignored them. The blue-prints to power and to at-

tainment have been uselessly held in his hands because he refused to exert the necessary faith to LIVE
the laws that he might KNOW of their power.

Any individual can begin to work miracles. The
first and greatest of all miracles will be those accomplished right within himself as he begins to fulfill the laws that he might *know* of their truth and
of their power. And as one seeks to prove them he
will advance from his mortal estate into a person
of eager, anticipating adventure. He will change
from a drab, perhaps uninteresting individual into
one alive and filled with an eagerness and a zest for
life—and that gift of life will become ever more
abundant.

Living the divine laws of fulfilment, and using
them constantly will set in motion a revolutionary,
exhilarating power of inner change. It will not be
discernable at first to mortal man. It will be felt.
And neither can it be boasted of for it is the sacred
unfolding of a man's own soul as it commences its
journey of complete fulfilment.

Noble aspirant for power and recognition, these
divine powers of Almighty God are but awaiting
your own fulfilment. They will be brought forth by
your own fulfilling as you increase in virtue and in
understanding and in light.

It takes effort, at first to lay down one's hates
and his small habits of character, that he has so
condoned and accepted he has failed to notice their
evil. He may not gossip or speak evil of his neighbor or bear false witness. He may only lend an ear

to gossip and thus encourage the repeater of scandal to carry the tale out to injure and to destroy, perhaps a life.

One may not commit adultery. But he may tell vile stories which increase and excite the lusts of his neighbor so that he will lose that divine control of his manhood.

One may speak no evil, he may only think it and feel it as he sends out his smoldering, wicked vibrations of resentment and hate.

One may not steal, yet in his proud, sabbatical self-righteousness he may cheat in his every dealing with his fellowmen.

The laws of righteousness are subtle and so easily ignored. One can "be a hearer of the word, but not a doer, and thus completely deceive himself."

Righteousness is not just a word. It is a way of life. It is a road of such dynamic power none has even begun to comprehend it. The human race has been a race of unawakened, self-satisfied mortals as they have moved slowly down their journey of life, impotent, dull and unprogressive.

Only in this day are men sufficiently awakened to throw off the swaddling clothes that have bound them and to rebel against the impotent diet of milk and soothing syrups that has satisfied them in a small measure. In this day the awakening is beyond anything that has happened in past ages. Men are not only demanding to *know the truth* but to KNOW God for themselves.

This awakened generation is a generation of sci-

entists and explorers who are willing to exert their
powers to check every method and every avenue,
to test and to try and to PROVE the things that
God has revealed, by LIVING them. This is a new
age and a new generation, such as the world has
never known. These dynamic ones, reserved from
the beginning to take their places in this day and
age, will not only span space and explore it, they
will fathom the atom and eventually its most intricate parts. And in the center of the atom they will
discover the dynamic power of God, for even the
atom is filled with spirit and with intelligence and
it too is being awakened to fulfill a greater role in
the plan of creation.

Man is now ready and prepared to explore the
great spiritual realm—and this divine exploration
must begin right within himself and in testing and
proving the promises which were revealed centuries
ago. And before this generation has passed away,
"A knowledge of the Lord will cover the earth even
as the waters cover the sea."

This age belongs to a generation such as has never
before been upon the earth. Oh, noble aspirants for
truth, I greet you in welcome as my soul yearns over
you in rapturous joy.

THE POWER TO BLESS AND HEAL

Chapter VIII

The most wicked and profane men on the earth bear more frequent witness to the divine Being of God than the righteous, though they would be the last to admit it. These violent men, with their uncontrolled thoughts and tongues, testify of God with almost every breath as they declare His name in their oaths and in their cursings. They, in their evil, are bearing witness of God as they continually call upon His name, in vain, for only in blessing can the name of God be used with power. He is a God of love and of blessings—and of good. And "they will not be held guiltless who taketh His name in vain."

To hear the name of God spoken with only a curse behind it is always a violent shock to the souls of the righteous. But it contains even a more violent and shattering effect upon those who pollute themselves and the earth with their blasphemy. Each blasphemous curse inflicts invisible wounds upon those who utter them. And these wounds and scars may take eons of time to heal. The untold damage these profane men are inflicting upon themselves is unbelievable and so pathetically tragic.

If only the righteous would think upon, and use, the name of God as constantly as the wicked and profane there would be no limit to the good they would accomplish.

If you have yearned for the opportunity to serve God, to be chosen by Him for service, then you will rejoice in the following information. The opportunity for you to serve is already at hand. And God is waiting anxiously for you to step into this divine service of eternal blessing. The opportunity has been so close few have ever beheld it. It has been too close at hand for man to lift his eyes to see, though Christ so plainly pointed it out.

This great, unheralded, silent service is so potent and so filled with power it is overwhelming and almost awesome when one opens up his heart to fulfill the greatness of such a divine and holy privilege of glory.

Begin to think upon the name of God and your eyes will become single to His glory. Use His name as frequently as the profane, only use it silently and with love and there will be no limit to the good you will accomplish. Use the name of God in blessing! Bless your neighbor! Bless and love him with a deep, compassionate love of infinite mercy. Shield him from scandal, even as you seek to defend your-

self from false, malicious gossip. Seek to justify his
shortcomings even as you so diligently, and sometimes blindly, seek to justify your own failings and
mistakes. Enfold your neighbor in love and, in the
name of God and His Beloved Son, Jesus Christ, pray
for him in sincere, loving solicitude.

Enlarge upon this great and Second Commandment as you apply it with power in your daily life.
Bless those you pass along the streets. Let no individual seem too insignificant, too unworthy or too
repulsive to receive the out-pouring of your blessings. Bless the crippled, the unfortunate and the erring and the proud and the arrogant. Bless those who
irritate you instead of disliking or resenting them.
Pray for every living soul. Pray and bless and pour
out your fullest quota of love until it becomes purified and unfeigned. Pray without ceasing. Fulfill
this divine law of the Second, Great Commandment
and you will grow into the dynamic service of Jesus
Christ in your complete fulness. Develop that divine
degree of love "that passeth understanding." As the
love of God begins to be poured out through your
heart you will have continual access to the fruit of
the Tree of Life, for "The fruit of the Tree of Life
is the love of God which is shed forth through the
hearts of the children of men."

Let this prayer of compassionate, tender love be
poured out constantly. Pray for all! Pray for the
rebellious, the defiant, the wicked and the seemingly
lost. Pray for those who have mistreated, persecuted, cheated or injured you in any way. Bless

them in the Name of the Lord! As you make use of
this divine power and privilege of prayer, silently,
unheralded and unacclaimed you will be entering
upon the works of Jesus Christ. This is the method
He was required to use at first in order to grow into
the services that were apparent.

You, like Christ, will not be permitted to behold
the good you accomplish in the beginning of your
labors, lest pride so fill your being you lose the way.
Yet this is the path of growth and of progress. It
is awaiting every individual on the earth who loves
God and who desires to serve.

As you pass, leaving your blessings behind you as
you go, you can also begin to send these blessings
of light out ahead of you to prepare the way before you. Those who use this love of constant blessing can never become self-righteous, bigoted or fanatical. It is the law that is so humbly and so un-
ostentatiously applied it is like the silent, loving
caress of the finger of God. It is like the passing
breath of an angel bringing healing and comfort
with it.

As you bless give thanks that God has heard your
silent requests. And in such blessings and in such
prayers you will be gathering the precious leaves
from that Sacred Tree of Life to help heal the nations. This is the greatest possible work one can be
engaged in at the present time. The nations consist
of the various races of men and the single individuals who make them up. As each recipient of your
blessings is, for a moment held within the loving,

enfolding embrace of your prayer, he is offered one of those precious leaves for his healing. He may not accept it. That is no concern of yours. You are to offer it. And the good of your offering may bear fruits "after many days."

This is the work of God that is awaiting your willing heart to undertake. This is your first assignment of divine service. This work is dynamic and powerful beyond the measure of your present capacity to comprehend until you have learned to live this law of outpouring love and eternal blessing.

These silent, whispered blessings are only released on the wings of your thoughts. They are not proclaimed aloud. This is a silent work of the soul as it steps forth to fulfill all the laws of righteousness. And through the fulfilling of this law is your physical body exalted and glorified for each blessing you release must first go through your own being.

Let your mind and thoughts caress mankind tenderly in a loving compassion as you pour out your constant benedictions to help heal and bless a world. Bless and rejoice always in your power to bless. This is the highway of joyous ecstasy and of thanksgiving and of eternal praise. This is the path of the righteous and of the neophyte who would become an "adept."

These silent, unacclaimed, unpronounced blessings were the first works which Christ performed. He practiced them for years before His public ministry began. And many of those whom He had blessed silently, in passing, were those who were awakened by that blessing to comprehend His teachings as He declared them aloud later.

This holy work of blessing must be done in silence, without show or self-righteousness taking control so that pride might be forever overcome. This is the only path of complete service.

This very power to bless silently, in the divine name of God, is a part of the training necessary for advancement. Bless without ceasing! Live with the name of God in your heart! Whisper it in your soul as you send out love! As you continue to use this silent power to bless, sending out only love and compassion, then will eventually follow the power to do the works which Christ did *openly*. The first steps toward power is along the silent, unheralded road of whispered blessings, poured out from the heart, with all the power and faith and love you can possibly exert. You will not be permitted to see the stupendous impact of your prayers in the beginning for you must first work from the heart, with a faith that has not yet become apparent.

As you travel this secret, inner road of blessings the good you will accomplish will reach far beyond your power to comprehend at the present time. But never doubt! Just bless and glorify God with every breath, and you will grow automatically into the greater powers. You will soon know fully what you are doing and what you will accomplish. And as you travel this divine highway of service and prayer you will realize that it is God who does the works.

And you will rejoice in the knowledge that He is using you as His divine instrument of blessing.

This constant power to bless and to love and to pray silently is even more of God's stupendous work than using these powers of creation to supply "your daily bread." The power to fulfill all your needs is only incidental. The power to bless and to forgive is the fulfilling of an everlasting, urgent, constant need, until the whole world is brought to "a knowledge of the Lord."

The moment anyone takes money for some spiritual service rendered he, in that moment, has closed the door to the power to supply his needs from the universal abundance. He is working for mammon and for the pay of the world. And those will be the wages he will receive. He has proved himself to be unworthy of his "higher" attainment.

As one fulfills these humble laws of divine, holy service, which cannot possibly be heralded, exploited, cashed in on, or even be retold, in order to appease his pride, he will speedily be prepared to serve more completely than he ever dreamed. He will, even as he offers his loving prayers of constant blessing, in a tender, unfanatical, loving outpouring of constant prayer, purify himself. And when he is completely purified he will not need to go out endeavoring to rend his desired blessings from heaven, nor to bring God's holy will down to his, nor to try to pry sanction and credits from those ahead of him on the road of attainment. The moment he has fulfilled all the laws and proved himself worthy

and ready all the powers and the blessings he has
prepared himself to receive will be his in their fulness. No one can demand these powers or blessings,
nor take them from another. Those who are rushing about, seeking to find someone to fulfill their
righteousness for them are wasting their time and
their divine powers of hope.

Those who are fulfilling the divine laws will not
rush out trying to entrap "flying saucers." Neither
will they intrude themselves upon those in high
places. When such have reached the heights of their
own preparation they will be *invited up*. Such will
never need to be invited down to take a lower seat.
They will be acknowledged fully and will be given
the powers that go with their own purification.

Humbly, silently and unknown to others must the
first works be accomplished. They are fulfilled
through silent prayer and continual blessings that
are released from the fulness of an adoring heart.
Only in this way can one be advanced to the status
of the approved. And only then will he be able to
perform the miracles, which only the true *"believers in Jesus Christ"* were promised the power to
accomplish. Such will be able to heal the sick,
cast out devils (or cure the insane), heal the halt,
the lame and the blind, and *raise the dead,* if such
be the will of God. In this higher service one does
nothing except God directs it. He speaks no word,
except God reveals it. In this complete obedience of
eternal power only the Will of God is accomplished
to the complete sanctification of him who serves.

This is how one becomes a servant in every deed.

As one grows into these higher powers now, unspeakable services will be accomplished for he will begin to do "all the works which Christ did." And then, he will *go on "to the greater works."* The full revelation of these greater works will be unfolded as one is prepared to perform them.

Such is the law of Christ, and the powers which govern His holy Light, which Light has been given to abide right within man.

You, most noble aspirant for service, know that your service can begin this instant as you commence to bless and continue to bless. Pray for those you meet along life's way. Pray for those who come to you from memory, whether they be living or dead. Bless those you meet along the streets, in a silent, loving compassion. Learn to feel towards them as God feels towards them in His great encompassing, understanding, forgiving mercy.

Bless and give thanks without ceasing. This is one of the major ways to begin to make use of the great Light of Christ until it becomes subject unto you. It must needs obey one as he develops it and brings it forth. It has always been man's to use only man did not know it. Now the keys of contacting that powerful, holy Light and of bringing it forth are fully revealed.

Use these keys humbly and constantly.

This very power, which has always been within your reach, has been the power which you have unconsciously yearned for God to bestow upon you.

It has remained concealed until you were sufficiently awakened to begin to seek and to search that you might KNOW God, instead of having someone tell you *about* Him.

This holy Light is the power that will purify, perfect and glorify you as you begin to use it silently, untrumpeted and unacclaimed, at first. This is the power you can begin to use with love and tenderness and infinite compassion to bind up the wounds of the broken (in spirit), and to heal the bodies and the minds of men. With this power released, through your constant prayers of praise and blessing, you will also have the power to begin to remove the scales of blindness from those who have never desired to see, for your light will begin to shine forth so that others seeing it will begin to glorify your Father, which is in heaven. They will not see that holy light with their physical eyes, not at first, for it will not be made thus apparent. But they will feel it. And they will begin to behold it with their spiritual eyes as your works of love bear witness of it in a joy of utter glory as it is released through you.

This is the power you can begin to use to help bring peace to the earth. Remember, your sincere, released blessings of compassion are the leaves from that sacred Tree of Life. And your love is the vehicle upon which they are carried forth, even to the bleak, the forelorn and the suffering and to the arid places of the earth, where it is most needed.

Such are the powers you now hold in your hands.

Use them graciously, humbly and continuously. Never tire of using them in your daily life that that life might unfold in fulfilling glory and infinite power.

This is the power of God in action as you begin to cooperate with Him. The developing and the bringing forth of these stupendous powers is up to you. These powers are unspeakable and tremendous beyond the knowledge of human thought. It is not possible to reveal their fulness to you now. You will be given the full understanding of them as you perfect yourself in their use. As you exercise your right to perfect this divine, holy power of prayer and blessing you will bring forth that Light even until you are "filled with Light and comprehend all things." And "all things will become subject unto you, both in heaven and on earth." "And nothing will be impossible to you" for such are the divine promises of Almighty God, through His Son, Jesus Christ.

In blessing continually "your mind and your lips will soon lose the power to hurt and wound. Then will your voice be heard among the Gods!" And such is your constant opportunity of service, right where you stand. And there is no person so alone and so unknown and insignificant who can not begin to use these divine powers as he begins "to evolve from the man kingdom into the God Kingdom."

This holy, divine service and this everlasting power is your divine heritage. And for this were you created. And this will be your glory as you begin to use the holy powers vested in you and the unutterable, incomprehensible privilege of prayer. Such are the dynamic powers of God awaiting your loving, compassionate, intelligent use of them. This instant! Every instant! There is no limit to the good you can accomplish. It is as limitless as the power of God is limitless.

Lift your eyes to His glory! Let them become single to that glory and watch yourself grow into it as your mortal weaknesses, shortcomings and failings drop away.

Oh, blessed one, as you LIVE these divine laws of blessing they will become your own for you will grow into them fully and completely. And in fulfilling these divine laws of silent, holy prayer you will fulfill the full measure of your own divinity. And know this surely and completely, that these prayers of blessing, as you send them forth, are truly "the prayers that are not be heard of men." They are for the ears of God only.

Beloved, noble aspirant for service, you need not seek on the outside for honors or acclaim or for rewards. They will be given to you from within. God's blessings are always from within as you become purified, ennobled, exalted and filled with light and eternal power. "Not as the world gives, give I unto you." You need only to fulfill the laws of your own inner being, the laws Christ so lovingly gave to the world. And as you fulfill them "Nothing will be impossible to you!"

In order that you might begin to comprehend and

to use these powers it will be necessary to reveal one more key that has been mentioned before, but not fully.

Trials are given for the perfecting of the individual that he might learn to develop his spiritual strength to the point where he can *stand forth* in that ancient acclamation and issue that all-powerful command, "Let there be Light!"

Each person has the right to command that Light to come forth, from right within himself, whenever overwhelming misfortunes or dismays or sorrows seek to submerge him or to silence his divine power of prayer.

As one knowingly issues that dynamic command, *"Let there be Light" within me,* he will be able to step aside and watch the fears and discords and confusion and the evils melt away as they are dissolved by that all-powerful vibration of Christ's holy Light.

This is another key by which that Light is brought into subjection to the individual along with that Celestial Song of Creation, the "New Song" of praise and love and gratitude, as well as the exercised privilege of blessing and praying without ceasing. These three methods contain the keys of all power and advancement and blessings. Each is a key in the life of him who would fulfill all the laws of righteousness, that all things might be added unto him.

This ability to command the "Light to stand forth" in all experiences and upon all occasions is stupendous in its power. This too is a key that can be used constantly as one learns to "walk in light." Or as the writer of those wonderful Odes of Solomon proclaimed; "I clothed myself in light, and acquired a body free from sorrow or affliction or pain."

As one learns to bring forth that divine Light from right within himself that "Light will become subject unto him." "All things will become subject unto him, both in heaven and on earth." And not only that light will become subject unto him *but the gift of life also*—*"and the Spirit and the Power,* sent forth by the will of the Father, through Jesus Christ, His Son."

As one offers his prayers of blessing and healing and enfolding love out to those he contacts, either in actuality or in memory, he will begin to bring forth that light. And within that power of prayer is the power to command the very gift of life itself. This is the power of healing in its fullest extent. And this is the promise of God to those who love and serve Him.

This divine, holy "Light of Christ is given to abide in *every man* who cometh into the world. And those who reject this Light (or who fail to bring it forth and use it) are under condemnation." They naturally remain in their impotent, grubby, mortal condition of endless vicissitudes that are the heritage of this "lone and dreary world" as they plod their bleak, unenlightened way to that desolate, back door —of death.

Up until now few have lifted their eyes to behold the great Light of the glory of God. And fewer still have held "their eyes single to that glory!" So very

few have *believed* sufficiently to go beyond the drab,
surface teachings of their creeds as they have trusted
in the arm of flesh instead of seeking to KNOW
God for themselves. These have indifferently relinquished their divine powers to "seek, to ask and
to knock," that they themselves might find God
and henceforth KNOW Him. But man is no longer
satisfied with the old-time religions that were good
enough for their ancestors and which are now as
out-moded as the covered wagons of the past.

New and wider frontiers have opened up in every
field of knowledge. Breathtaking accomplishments
have been achieved in every field of learning to
which man has directed his mind. And the result
has been unbelievable as each stupendous door opened has revealed breathtaking new fields to explore.

Now, the most exciting field of all research has
opened wide its doors. It is the spiritual field! The
unexplored realm of the soul of man and his right
to actually KNOW God.

In this stupendous new search to find a man's
soul and to KNOW God, not through hear-say, but
by individual accomplishment it is discovered that
each individual is equipped with a laboratory in
which he can test, for himself, every formula and
every teaching—and ascertain which are of God
and which are of men. Each person is given the
necessary equipment and the intelligence and the
dynamic, unspeakable power to prove for himself
every word and every promise ever given by God
to man. And man himself is the testing ground for

every word Christ ever uttered. And never before have the doors to that spiritual realm been opened so wide and so invitingly for man to step forth and fulfill the full measure of his own creation.

The keys of infinite power and spiritual understanding have remained unrevealed for centuries because of man's willingness to accept whatever he was told without testing its power. He has been satisfied to blindly follow, the blind leaders who have lead him. So has man been cheated and his soul robbed and he has fallen with his brothers, into the ditch of death.

The dynamic keys of power and of complete knowledge are now made in fulfilment to God's holy promises from the very beginning of time. The *"Great and unspeakable things which God has hid up from the foundation of the world, because of the* GROSS WICKEDNESS OF UNBELIEF,"* are now opened and available to all who desire them.

These stupendous truths and powers have been awaiting a generation who would no longer be satisfied with an insipid diet of milk and spewed out vomit. This age belongs to those who have awakened to the desolating pangs of a spiritual hunger that can no longer be appeased by the powerless creeds and formulas of the past. These awakened ones are "hungering and thirsting after *righteousness,"* not platitudes or appeasements or powerless doctrines. These are the ones who must satisfy that yearning hunger to KNOW by fulfilling the command to "ask, to seek and to knock."

These awakened ones will no longer be restrained by the secular authorities, who are but blocking the way. These noble ones are already seeking both "early and diligently" that they might know Him, the only true and living God, and Jesus Christ, whom He has sent!" These great, advancing, spiritual sons of God will never again be satisfied with the dead conformity to earthly ritualism. They can no more return to the dead, unprogressiveness of their fore-fathers than a jet pilot or an astronaut would be willing to travel in an ancient camel caravan or with a covered wagon, drawn by a plodding ox team.

These awakening ones are at last aware that the leaders, who lulled them to sleep with their professed knowledge, are themselves blind. These enlightened ones are no longer interested in being informed *about* God. They are reaching to KNOW God. "And to know Him is life eternal."

This very promise of eternal life is based on man's search to know God for himself. This search is as necessary to man's divine progress as the principle of birth is necessary to commence one's sojourn in mortality.

And as one lives the laws of God he will KNOW of their truth and of their power. He will need none to tell him. And the promise is to all: "Those who seek me diligently shall find Me!"

This is the day of spiritual awakening! This is the beginning of the day of power. This is the day of God Almighty and every individual will have a part in it whether he is prepared or not. Yet all are invited to participate in the great glory of this wondrous day—a day such as has never been before or ever will be again. For those who are prepared it is a day of unspeakable glory. For those who are unprepared it will be a day of regret and of deep sorrow.

Thank God that you are privileged to live in this great day—the day of the consumation—of the fulfilling—of the ending and the beginning of all that was or will be.

"LAY HOLD OF THE BEST GIFTS!"

Chapter IX

Faith is born and fulfilled out of the *impossible*. Only the *impossible* gives a meaning and a reason to the stupendous principle and power of faith.

Paul gave the admonition: "Lay hold of the best gifts!" The best gifts are the spiritual powers and gifts of God.

One can have all the wealth possible to possess and only fulfill the words given in the third chapter of Revelations, which states: "Because thou sayest, I am rich, and increased with goods and have need of nothing; and knowest not that thou art wretched, and miserable and poor and blind and naked; I counsel thee to buy of me gold tried in the fire, that thou mayest be rich; and white raiment, that thou mayest be clothed, and that the shame of thy nakedness do not appear; and anoint thine eyes with eyesalve, that thou mayest see."

"The gold tried in the fire" is the spiritual gold.
This priceless, golden treasure of unspeakable worth
is situated at the place of contact with God and
with His marvelous, unlimited source of creation.
It is situated at the very center of each man's soul.
It is a spiritual substance, liquid, molten and supersensitive. Every doubt and every negatious vibration,
every evil desire or uncontrolled, mortal reaction
keeps it in a state of storm-tossed turbulence. As
this turbulence reflects out its confusion that distorted image is brought back into an individual's
life as evils, dismays, illness, poverty or troubles of
one sort or another. The great power of this priceless gift of gold is bestowed when one learns to become "still," when his emotions are controlled by
love and when his doubts are conquered by the exerted principle of learning to "believe." When this
is accomplished then one purchases the "gold that
has been tried in the fire" of his own testings.

Or, as James gave it in his first chapter: "Know
that the *trying* of your faith worketh patience. But
let patience have her perfect work, that ye may be
perfect and entire, wanting nothing." The man who
has perfected that hallowed gift of patience can
easily obtain "The gold that has been tried in the
fire." In his soul is the quieted peace that can hold
that spiritual gold in a perfection of equilibrium
or "stillness" that will bring forth his completion
and the fulfilment of all his righteous desires so
that "he will lack for nothing."

James goes on to describe the storm-tossed tur-

bulence that comes when one wavers or doubts, thus
failing to "lay hold of the gifts and blessings" he
most desires.

"If any of you lack wisdom, let him ask of God,
that giveth to ALL men liberally and upbraideth
not; *and it shall be given him.* But let him ask in
faith, nothing wavering (no changing or doubting).
For he that wavereth is like a wave of the sea driven
by the wind and tossed. For let not that man think
that he shall receive anything of the Lord."

Here James has given a description of the great
gift God has offered, the "gold tried in the fire,"
that must be "stilled" by patience, by love and by
a constant awareness of the deepest desires one holds
in his heart. He even describes the turbulence of
that storm-tossed sea and the impossibility of God
granting any blessing to the person who fails to fulfill the great law of purchasing that precious gold,
the molten gold of eternal glory in which the powers
of creation are held.

As one holds his mind, unwaveringly and without
doubts upon any great desire or "best gift" that gold
solidifies and holds the pattern or design of ones request out to reflect its commands upon the very
"atoms waiting to become."

It is in this *"stilled"* mirror of molten gold, at
the center of one's soul, that all wants and all desires are reflected out into the universal "substance
of things hoped for." This is the method by which
the "things hoped for" are brought forth into tangible form or fulfilment. This pool, or mirror of

molten gold, when not "tried in the fire" reflects out quite as readily all the evil emotions, doubts, fears and negatious evils in a mass of contorted reflections that bring back nothing but ills. "For let not that man think he shall receive anything of the Lord." Not that the Lord is not willing and anxious to bestow all gifts and blessings upon him, but he has refused to use the law of their coming forth and of his own powers to use his divine heritage of creation correctly. Each man is fully equipped with the powers of creation, few have learned to use them "RIGHTEOUSLY" for they are the laws of righteousness. "All that the Father has is yours."

To comprehend and to use these great powers of creation or that "Kingdom of Heaven" righteously is power indeed. And within it is contained the eternal promise of God that one will receive all else, and the fulfilment of every need, even before he asks. This is wealth indeed. And with this source of supply opened there can be no want. Neither can any cares nor fears nor worries over the rust, the moths, the thieves and the adverse conditions of failures in business, or banks, or professional deals, or what-have-you be able to destroy the supply of eternal good.

This place of high, spiritual "gold that has been tried in the fires" of one's own soul and in his own testings, is situated at the very center of man's own being. It is located before the throne of that "Inner Kingdom," of which Christ spoke. And he who seeks this inner contact and establishes that contact is

rich indeed. For then only can one receive the gold
that has been tried in the fire and which holds the
power to fulfill every righteous desire and every
worthy request. "Thus all things will be added unto
him, both in heaven and on earth." "He will never
again need to labor for the things that perish."
Neither will he ever again "hunger or thirst."

Within this great source of creation is contained
the material blessings that can never be lost or with-
drawn. But even more important are the great spiritual powers and blessings that have been ignored because they have not been apparent to the mortal,
dense, physical senses.

Such are the gifts which Paul admonished men
to lay hold of. The best gifts are always intangible
to the physical mind until they are completely established. And it is because they are not at first visible
or apparent to the earthly senses that one must learn
to "lay hold of them," not with his hands, but with
his mind, then with his heart and with his soul.
Then they become his own.

Any individual who can lift his mind to "lay hold"
of any spiritual gift *until he no longer doubts in his
heart, but believes that he receives he shall have
whatsoever he asks.* The gift is given spiritually first.
And his soul will KNOW that he has received it.
All things were created spiritually first, even the
earth itself—and every herb before it grew.

As one holds his mind unwaveringly and without
doubting upon any gift or desire that sea of molten
gold solidifies and the pattern of his request is estab-

lished as it is reflected out for those celestial rays of living light to fulfill. These illimitable rays are turned upon themselves as they are drawn into the mold or pattern reflected out from that molten gold, or mirror. Thus are they formed into atoms and are gathered to fulfill the need, the request or the desire held out to them, unwaveringly. These rays of living light are "the substance of things hoped for" as they are formed into atoms and congealed into material form. This is the spiritual process and power of creation. And it is man's to use. "All that the Father has is yours!" Even the power of creation.

James was not permitted, in his time, to reveal the full truth of the law of asking without wavering. Christ only pointed the way to its fulfilling by giving the information that if one *lived the laws* he would *know* of their truth and of their power. But only now has the veil been completely removed that each man might be left without excuse. The way is his own.

This undoubting condition of the heart, that is required for fulfillment, may not be an easy condition to achieve at first. But there is no man living who cannot achieve this condition of complete fulfilment if he has not destroyed his ability to *believe* by his continual effort to *"disprove* all things."

First, it is necessary to "lay hold of these *best* gifts" with the mind, by thinking of them, desiring them and beginning to live worthy of them. These gifts are spiritual and as one develops the desire for them, by holding them in his thoughts, then goes on to the point where he can ask God for them, he is on the path of fulfilment. If he continues to "ask, to seek and to knock," the law of heaven is fulfilled and therefore must bring the fulfilling of such requests into complete consumation.

Again, let me quote a portion of the ninth Command, given to Hermas, by the angel, which is as follows: "Again he said unto me; remove from thee all doubting; and question (or doubt) nothing at all, when thou asketh anything of the Lord; saying within thyself: how shall I be able to ask anything of the Lord and receive it, seeing I have so greatly sinned against him?

"Do not think thus, but turn unto the Lord with all thy heart, and ask of him without doubting, and thou shalt know the mercy of the Lord; how that he will not forsake thee, but will fulfill the request of thy soul.

". . . Do not leave off to ask, and then thou shalt receive. Else if thou shalt cease to ask, thou must complain of thyself, and not of God, that he has not given unto thee what thou didst desire." (Lost Books of the Bible. II Hermas: Command IX:1-2 & 7).

To "lay hold of" anything demands that one reach for it and then cling to it until he establishes his right of ownership or possession. To "lay hold of the best gifts" or the great spiritual blessings one must lay hold of them with his thoughts until he establishes a desire for them in his heart. This will establish his claims and imprint his desires upon that mirror of pure gold—"the gold that has been tried in the fire."

This pool of pure, spiritual gold is contained in the great glory of that divine, *inner stillness* as one closes the door of his attention, or closet, to all outside turmoil and confusion and distractions. In the divine *stillness* of supreme quietude one will find the contact with God. In this inner quieting and stillness one learns to hear the voice of God as he begins to receive personal instruction from the Almighty. In this divine center "The Holy Spirit of Promise" reveals the great possibilities ahead, waiting fulfilment. As one learns to enter into and abide in this center of great peace, "The peace that passeth understanding," he is abiding in God, or in that divine contact with him.

As one learns to enter into and to abide in this great *stillness,* the point of *peace* and *power,* that divine pool of pure, molten glory is held in perfect tranquility so that no ripple of disquietude or unbelieving doubts can mar its surface to shatter the reflection one places into it by his own inspired desiring. Only through this great treasure of inner, molten gold, that has been tried in the fire, can one possibly receive back the perfect answer to his inner longings. As the pool of pure, spiritual gold is held in *stillness,* it reflects out into the universal "substance of things hoped for", the exact pattern of one's desires. In the great *stillness* the desires of the heart are held forth in such vivid clarity their very power draws back the divine elements of complete fulfilling.

As long as doubts or discords or any negative condition or traits are permitted to exist there is only a crazy, broken pattern sent out upon the disturbed ripples or turbulent surface of that pool. And thus one receives only the most skimped, mediocre returns for his longings. He perhaps receives back only his own shattered dreams, his broken health and a life of drab, purposeless living—a mere existence.

"Buy of me the gold that is tried in the fire that thou mayest be rich."

How do you buy it?

By learning to "be still—and *know* God." "Be Still" and become acquainted with His great, dynamic power of creation and the method of using it—for this is the "Kingdom of heaven, that is within." Seek this Kingdom and its righteousness and all else will be added unto you."

To those who fulfill the laws of this great righteousness there is no power in existence which can withhold the fulfilling of their requests, no matter how seemingly impossible they may appear to be.

Only in righteousness can this law of creation be used. But when one becomes proficient in the knowledge and the virtues of using these dynamic powers his requests will be answered instantly, for, "Before they ask I will answer." At the beginning time is required to perfect the individual and his faith. After one learns how to use the law in righteousness he will have the power to move mountains, raise the dead, and do all that Christ did, then go on to the greater works.

The power of prayer is dynamically potent with the eternal forces of Almighty God. But to use the power of prayer one must send it out from the very depths of his heart with the strength of his soul carrying it forth on the wings of love and praise and gratitude. This method opens the inner realm of one's being and *stills* that pool of molten gold.

It is most assuredly true that any one who learns to "lay hold of any gift" or blessing or desire and continues to "ask and seek" for its fulfilment, will receive, "for everyone who asks receives and he who seeks finds and unto him who knocks it shall be opened," even that inner realm of his own soul in which the powers of contact with Almighty God are held. This is the "Secret place of the Most High," the center of a man's own soul, the "Kingdom of heaven within."

And it is true that prayer can and will change the pray-er. As one "lays hold" of any gift or desire and continues to pray for it, first with his mind, the energies of his heart and soul will finally take up that petition and it will become an established reality. First it is established in the spiritual realm from which all material things are originally formed, then, by the law of its own fulfilment it will become a fact and a true reality in the tangible realm of material existence.

"There is *nothing impossible* to God!" There is *nothing impossible* to the person who aligns himself with God. As one gets in contact with that inner realm, or "Kingdom of heaven within," he gets in contact with the spiritual realm out of which all existing things are formed—the things both in heaven and on earth.

It is impossible to reach too high or to desire too much as long as one wishes these exquisite, dynamic powers and blessings to help benefit a world, or wishes them to use for the service of man. Only in righteousness can these powers be used. Never in selfishness nor for evil. He who seeks to use them thus will himself be destroyed.

However, no one can follow this inner road of prayer without himself being purified and changed into "a new being" worthy and prepared to be entrusted with such divine gifts and powers. This road of prayer is not performed in the telling of beads nor in habitual mutterings. This road of prayer must come from the soul with all the energies of the heart sending it out. And this method of prayer will open the heart and reveal fully the great glories contained within the soul.

"Lay hold of the best gifts" and begin to "ask, to seek and to knock" and never cease to lay claim or to hold to the desire of your heart and it will be fulfilled unto you. This is the law—and it is irrevocable.

This liquid, molten pool of gold, in which one's sincere requests or heart desires are reflected and mirrored out into the universal realm holds the entire method of creation. Again I am instructed to stress the information that in the reflected vision held out onto the surface of that pure gold the atoms or elements of "the substance of things hoped for," is gathered into tangible form. Those living rays of pure, spiritual light are drawn to it, turned upon themselves to form atoms and those atoms will be solidified into the physical or tangible substance of that which is held out to them to fulfill.

This is the law of creation. It is as eternal as eternity and as unfailing and unchangeable as God. The law is that the spiritual substance of "things hoped for" must obey the law of existence as it is gathered and molded into the form or pattern held forth for fulfilment. This is the working method of the law of creation and the method of applying it in one's daily life. This is the kingdom of righteousness, in which all needed things are added.

When it states in Genesis that God formed this, or that, or the other, then *saw* that it was good it is stating that He held His mental vision upon the idea until it was completely formed or fulfilled. This is the law of the inner working of faith. And it is the law God used in creating this world and the planets and all existing things thereof. It is the only method of creation. And never before on this earth has the fulness of this breathtaking, dynamic law of fulfilment been revealed. It has been "one of those great, unspeakable truths that was hidden up from the foundation of the world, because of the great wickedness of unbelief!" It was not even known in the Estate of Eden.

It is now revealed because the promise is: "When men would *rend that veil of unbelief,* which has caused the world to remain in its awful state of wickedness" this knowledge would be revealed.

There are those, in this day and age, who have so desired to KNOW truth and to KNOW GOD for themselves that the veil of darkness is being rent to the extent that some of these stupendous truths of eternity are beginning to come forth. See that you mock them not, for God will not be mocked!

Fulfill these laws of faith and of creation and prove them for yourself. Cast your doubting and your unbelief from you. And as you love and praise and give thanks with ever increasing power you will be given the full knowledge of the working of these unspeakable laws. You will be "clothed in the white raiment" or in the glorious Light of Christ so that your mortal nakedness of impotency will never appear.

"Anoint your eyes with eye salve that you might see" "with eyes single to the glory of God" and you will begin to take upon you that glory, or to reflect it. The law of reflecting, or of mirroring out is a dynamic law. It is the method by which atoms are formed from the universal substance of vibrant, spiritual light. It is the only method that can be used to work with atoms, either for creation or for the releasing of the energy contained within them. The scientists use mirrors to an almost incomprehensible extent as they explode the atoms in a series of chain reactions.

"All that the Father has is yours," even the dynamic power of creation as you seek for the Kingdom of God and its righteousness, where all else will be added unto you. These higher laws of creation can only be used by those who have begun to evolve from the man kingdom of greed and grabbing and selfishness and evils and lusts into the God Kingdom.

The law of the angels has been partially explained. This added information is the law of Gods, the dynamic law of creation.

At the beginning of creation God's first command, in the process of bringing forth, was: "LET THERE BE LIGHT!" And it was from those living rays of Light that all tangible things were created or formed. James proclaimed it in his first chapter as he designated God, "The Father of Lights!" It is from God that the rays of living light are sent out in a fathomless stream of unending, dynamic, eternal flowing.

I BEAR WITNESS TO THE TRUTH

Chapter X

"Pray without ceasing!" Pray and your prayers will be answered! Pray during every, unoccupied moment of living. Pray in your wakeful periods of night. Pray whenever the thought comes to you and you will develop the ability to make that prayer so potent your soul will take it up and send it out even when your mind is still occupied with the necessary tasks of your mortal life. And when the soul finally takes up that prayer or request the fulfilment is at hand.

There is nothing impossible! The only thing that is impossible is to reach too high or to desire too much! As "your eyes become single to the glory of God" your desires will be purified and exalted to that glory and embrace the powers Christ used and which He promised to all those who would only believe on Him. He established "the path, which so

few have found" because they look on the outside,
expecting to find someone else who will travel it
for them.

In Christ's parable of the man who went to his
neighbor, at night, to obtain bread to feed an un-
expected guest, and in the story of the widow and
the judge, He established forever the method of receiving the answer to one's prayers or requests—
the method of continued asking. It isn't that God
either requires or desires His children to beg in anguish and tearful pleading. It is only that by the
praying the individual himself is purified and prepared to receive all that God can possibly bestow,
even until there is not room enough to receive.

So "few find His Path" because so many are unwilling to LIVE the laws He gave. It takes energy
and exerted effort to mold oneself into the pattern
required for fulfilment, or at least it appears to be
so to the person who loves the laws of the flesh and
his own weaknesses. To those burdened with their
worldly interests and earthly desires it seems to be
much easier to sit back and wish for another to do
the fulfilling for them, even if they lift their vision
high enough to glimpse the higher way.

Each person must do his own fulfilling. This is
the law. It is the only method of progress in existence.

Reason and I were removed from all personal
contact with individuals, for a period of time, because too many were seeking to take hold of us,
expecting us to do their fulfilling for them. Such

can never receive their own full measure of accomplishment—not worlds without end.

Such ideas of expecting others to carry the burden of one's own purification is not only retarding but completely out of line with one's own development. Those who insist upon rushing to and fro in a determined effort to receive their exaltation will find only humiliation and disappointment. They are attempting to fill the high seats they have not earned and will "be invited down" which is extremely humiliating.

None need to reach to others for fulfilment. Each individual has the complete path of his own divine progress, his own fulfilling right within himself. This is the divine, inner path of his own beautiful purification and righteousness as he seeks for that sublime Kingdom of Heaven. But the search is his own.

Just as soon as any individual reaches the measure of his own inner purification God Himself will place His own seal of approval upon him, and like Enoch of old, he will receive the witness or testimony that God is pleased with him. Nothing else matters. The approval and sanction of men is meaningless and misleading.

Each individual must lay hold of the things which would be "The best gifts" according to his own degree of understanding and advancement. And each must hold to those gifts until he has brought that inner glory of himself forth in preparation to be able to receive "all that the Father has!"

Let your mind reach out to contemplate the wonders and the glories of God! Then set your mind upon the gifts or blessings you desire to receive, and thus lay hold of them. Begin to "ask and to seek" and to "pray without ceasing." Yes. "Pray with all the energy of heart" and the power of faith will be established and fulfilled unto you and nothing will be impossible! This is the method of *"exercising great and mighty faith."* Use it and the power will become your own.

Now, another truth I am instructed to unfold. The world has stood back in awed, almost overwhelming breathlessness as mankind has contemplated the powers and the miracles and the works of the great spiritual leaders of the past. Yet none have ventured to lift their eyes to behold "The glory of God" else they too would have aspired to achieve as much as those ancient prophets and apostles and inspired ones of days gone by.

YOU can be as great and accomplish as much as any individual who ever lived upon the earth, YOU can do the works which Christ did, "Even greater works." Do you believe this? If not then you do not believe Him. But you can prove His words, if you have a mind to do so. Live the laws and you will KNOW!

"God is no respecter of persons." Any individual who will fulfill the laws of righteousness will be given the powers that pertain to righteousness. This is not self-righteousness. This is the reaching of that Kingdom of Heaven, within. Fulfill the laws which the ancients fulfilled, by loving God with all your heart, your mind and your soul and strength, and pray without ceasing as you hold your eyes single to the glory of God and you will take on that same glory and receive of His powers. You will be able to accomplish anything and everything your heart can possibly desire in righteousness.

Worship and adore without ceasing. And in your devotion see that you worship no man. Worship God only.

In the twenty-second chapter of Revelations, verses eight and nine, John bore record of this important truth in the following words: "And I John saw these things, and heard them. And when I had heard and seen, I fell down to worship at the feet of the angel which showed me these things.

"Then said he unto me, See thou do it not: for I am thy fellow servant, and of thy brethren the prophets."

Always the admonition has been, "Worship God! And Him only must you serve!" In the very beginning of *time* this command was given in love and solicitude: "Do all that you do in the Name of the Lord, and call upon the Name of the Son forevermore!" This was the key by which mankind could reclaim its lost estate, but few followed the admonition. Enoch was one of those who fulfilled the greatness of those instructions and passed beyond mortality.

And now I am instructed to bear witness to the truth of this work, though I became an outcast because of my testimony.

When the book "Ye Are Gods" was scheduled to come forth I spent many anguished hours pleading with God to have someone important write that glorious record. My tears flowed continually as I wrote for that work was written in fire and tears. At first the burden of my prayer was, "Dear God, please let someone else write these truths—someone important! Almighty Father, let someone in authority write it! I could accept it if I found it in the gutter! I would love it if I found it soiled with sewer dirt and wrapped in slime."

Then came the powerful impact of His words as He answered, "That is why you have been chosen and ordained to write my message."

And now, I bear solemn witness, in the Name of Jesus Christ and before the world, that these books were written under the direction and power of God and according to His command. I did not wish to place my name upon them but those who would condemn had to have someone whom they could revile against and accuse. For that reason alone is my name upon these books.

As stated before, that first record was written in fire and tears as the Light of God poured through my being and out through my fingertips upon the pages placed in the typewriter. My soul worshipped and adored in a humble relinquishment of self during those days of writing.

The calouses upon my knees alone bore witness to the days and months I had spent upon my knees to *know* truth, long before this work was begun. Nor could those who have never exerted themselves to understand the marvelous workings of God know how the things I had studied in the past, the great truths I had searched for, fell into place like the intricate pieces of a great jig-saw puzzle, as I wrote. It took years of study to gather into my mind and heart those dynamic truths. It took but thirty days for God to bring forth in revealing, living light and arrange them in a volume as great as "Ye Are Gods."

And now, I bear witness also that I lay no claim to this work of revealing glory. I offer no apology for it. I do not retract it in order to appease the ego of those who reject that which is sent through the weakest and most foolish of His Children, according to His words. I only bow my head in reverent adoration and gratitude that my hands could touch anything as wonderful as the things God has permitted me to write. If I could have made a choice of all the things on this earth I would most like to do, I would answer without hesitation, "I would rather have been privileged to write a book as divinely beautiful as "The Celestial Song of Creation" than do anything else in this world.

Of myself I could not have written these books in a lifetime of searching and striving. I came from a talented family yet the only gift I received was a good memory. That memory was used as the things I had studied in a lifetime of hungry searching were unfolded in the flames of God's dynamic light as they fell into place in a record of revealing truth.

And if God chose me, the least, the most unlearned, the most foolish and unwise and the weakest of all His children to be His scribe I can no longer protest for I was told that that was no concern of mine—that I was to write.

And so I wrote. Under His direction I wrote even as He directed. And I understood the great, dynamic truths as I wrote them, for the power of the inner meanings were revealed even as I wrote. And often I would pray, "Dear God, how can I write these things? They are almost impossible to even think? And who will be able to receive them, and who read them?" I was informed, when the first book was being written that it was to be a "great volume" and would go out to the whole world. And when I felt that I could not possibly write those dynamic truths I was told not to concern myself about who would receive it or who read it because it belonged entirely to God.

And so I could accept no pay or receive no royalties for these sacred books. They were not mine. I could lay no claim to them, except that I had been called to be the scribe.

And those who condemned me for so great a work offered me continued membership in their church, in which I had served with all my strength, my time and talents and financial means and power for years and in which my ancestors before me had served for five generations, if I would proclaim that I had erred in my writing and testify that God had nothing to do with the work. How could I bear false witness against God or against that which He

had commanded me to write as His words had
poured out through my mind and my body and my
hands like living fire as I wrote? How could I betray Him thus?

And so I bear witness before the world that this
work is true and that every word and every promise
contained within these books will be fulfilled unto
all those who will only humble themselves to ask of
God, then live the laws contained therein that they
might KNOW for themselves.

He who says it is wicked to love God with all his
heart, mind, soul and strength is himself in the thrall
of wickedness. He who protests that man is not to
believe and fulfill Christ's most holy injunction, "Be
ye therefore perfect, even as your Father in heaven
is perfect," knows nothing of truth. For God has
said, "I give no commandment save I prepare the
way for its fulfilment." And Christ Himself said,
"Anything which enticeth a man to pray and to
love and serve God is of God." Those who deny
these truths have no truth in them. And they are
the blind who continue to lead the blind along that
mortal road which leads to death.

Those who love God and those who believe in
Jesus Christ, His Divine, Beloved Son, comprehend
that His entire mission on the earth was to bestow
"The life more abundant" upon man. And "Life
Eternal" was offered as the complete fulfilment of
the law that man need not die. This was the great
revelation He came to give and these were His holy,
dynamic promises. This Path of life is the Path He

marked, even as He traveled it—and left His precious map that man could follow if so they would
desire.

"Cursed is he who trusts in the arm of flesh; or
maketh flesh his arm." "Worship God only and
serve only Him!" Hold no man in awe, nor worship
him. He is but your fellow servant regardless of his
own esteem of himself.

Worship God and know that within you is the
power to actually KNOW GOD, instead of just
knowing about Him. And know also that you can
accomplish all that has ever been accomplished as
you open your heart to purification by releasing a
constant prayer of praise and love and gratitude.
As you prepare yourself thus God will be able to
use you in whatsoever capacity you are prepared to
fill.

To love and praise and give thanks is the method
of purification and of accomplishment and of fulfilment. You can fulfill every law of every church
and every creed, all the "dos and the don'ts" and
the most minute, strict interpretation of the laws by
just living those two Great and glorious Commandments of Love. And in living these two laws you not
only fulfill all others, you go beyond them. Perfect
the gift of love and you will have continual access
to the very fruit of the Tree of Life, and you will no
longer be under their law. Thus you can fulfill the
command to "leave the first principles of the Gospel,
of faith, repentance and baptism and the laying on
of hands, and go on unto perfection!"

Look to no man to help you in your fulfilment, for as you "ask, seek and knock" God Himself will become your instructor and His Spirit will be poured out upon all (of your) flesh until even your physical body will be exalted and glorified in the "Life more abundant." And thus you will be lifted beyond the mortal claims of a physical world as you "evolve from the man kingdom into the God Kingdom."

Praise and give thanks continually, without ceasing. "Ask, seek and knock" and you will be prepared to receive the power to accomplish your own great destiny as God accepts you as a chosen instrument in His hands. And nothing will be impossible unto you." Such are the eternal, irrevocable, almighty promises of God the Father, Creator of heaven and of Earth and of all that in them are."

These great truths have never before been revealed in their fulness. James was not permitted to unfold the great law of faith nor the meaning of the waves which would leave one empty and devoid of his requests.

Christ only pointed the way by promising that any who would LIVE the laws He gave would KNOW of their truth.

Only now, in this day, has the intricate, perfect working of the law of faith and of creation been fully revealed, and the full law of righteousness. LIVE these laws of Jesus Christ — and you will KNOW!

————————

And now I bear witness that I understood exactly what I was writing as God enlightened my mind with the divine Light of understanding. I bear witness that I did not write by any power taking over my mind or directing my hand. I did not write while in a trance as some have supposed and proclaimed. I wrote under the power of Almighty God and according to His direction and the truths that were recorded were His truths.

So be it known.

THE CHURCH OF THE FIRSTBORN

Chapter XI

The laws of the "Church of the Firstborn" are the laws written upon the sacred, inner tablets of man's own heart. They contain the innermost knowledge of his own divine soul. These eternal laws or this sublime record of glory embraces the complete truth of each man's being.

As one learns to feel these dynamic truths he will soon begin to comprehend or to *"know* truth." And in the application of this knowledge *"he will become free."*

This inner law contains a knowledge of what each man was in the beginning, what he *now* is and what he can become as his own exalted pattern of life is made manifest in all the magnificent wisdom and love of the Almighty Creator. In this all-inclusive unfolding of the great, individual truth is contained the eternal revelation of "the great truth" or "all truth." And in this contact is contained the wondrous revelation of each man's destiny or individual assignment as it is made apparent. Each individual was given an honorable commission to fulfill before ever he came to earth.

This revelation of the past, as one at last opens his mind to recall his own pristine glory, as a child of light, is not some skimped little idea of having been someone important in a previous re-incarnation. It has nothing to do with the idea that he was, at some time, in a previous, mortal life a very important person. Only very mediocre people have such vain-glorious ideas. And it is always those who are farthest from fulfilling their own high, divine destinies who console themselves with the idea that they were someone quite important in another lifetime.

Right now, right where they stand, if they would but fulfill the law of their own beings, they would be as great as they could possibly imagine themselves being. In their present journey they are all that they ever were or ever could possibly hope to be only they do not know it. And because of the gross blindness that covers the earth and veils their minds they fail to seek a knowledge of that truth.

THIS life, right now, is the one appointed for each man to discover his own greatness and to contact God that he might fulfill every possibility of himself. Within each individual is contained the potentialities of all the greatness, all the love and all the power possible for him or her to receive and to glorify. It is up to each individual to "know the truth" of himself and to glorify God with that divine contact which brings that holy "at-one-ment."

Each person is indeed important in his or her own right, as a child of Light, off-spring of the Almighty, brought forth in sublime perfection, with an individual destiny of eternal glory awaiting fulfilment.

Those who "seek first the Kingdom of God and its righteousness" will have all things added unto them. And in this knowledge will be the unfolding of their own divinity and inherent powers.

Those who, of themselves, seek for the dynamic "Kingdom of Righteousness" will refuse to permit themselves to be blocked by earthly ritualism and empty conformities. Such searching ones will develop the great "hungering and thirsting after righteousness" which will demand that that *hungering* be appeased. And the appeasement of this divine hungering can only find appeasement in an actual contact with God.

Those who refuse to be fed upon the crumbs of knowledge, or upon the weak, insipid diet of milk must go on until they behold the face of Christ and are then admitted into membership into His True Kingdom, which is not of this world. This is the "Kingdom of the Firstborn" and consists of "the Great Brotherhood of Light."

This higher "Kingdom, which is not of this world," is symbolized by every church and creed. And those who are still infants and who have not yet awakened themselves to "ask and to seek and to knock" will

be satisfied with his toys as he continues to dwell in
the land of make-believe.

Those who have not developed the true "hungering and thirsting after righteousness" are the ones
who are satisfied with the childish trappings and
with an infant's diet of milk.

For those who are *seeking* both early and diligently to KNOW God for themselves, the great
"hungering and thirsting" becomes acute and in
its intensity it must find appeasement.

Too long has man slept in his infant crib of conformity, wrapped in the swaddling clothes of mortal
teachings. Truly the crib has become so short one
cannot stretch himself in it, nor is he expected to.
Nor can he raise himself from his impotent position
to behold clearly either his surroundings or his own
status.

The time has come when man must awake and
arise! He must climb out of his outgrown bed and
discard the covering that has become too narrow
to either give him warmth or comfort or hide the
shame of his nakedness.

By his own efforts man must cast aside the childish
trappings of infancy and step out toward his own
divine maturity. And those who desire to go beyond
the infant stage of impotency into the state of power
must develop the great "hungering and thirsting after
righteousness" that cannot be appeased with anything less than actually *KNOWING GOD!* And
this is life eternal, which Christ came to give.

It is time for man to step out of the infant stage

of pacifiers and soothing syrups and childish lullabies and the weak, insipid milk diet of babies into
his own divine manhood of actually KNOWING
for himself. It is indeed time for him to reach for
the food that will give him the power "to grow and
wax strong!"

The "hungering and thirsting after righteousness,"
which holds the power of one's own completion and
fulfilment, must be developed through an inner
reaching as one learns to turn constantly to God in
a devotion of singing praise and earnest, loving
prayer.

And the law is: that he who develops this great
inner "hungering and thirsting" to actually KNOW
truth and to KNOW God that hungering must be
appeased. This is the law of God: "Blessed are those
who hunger and thirst after righteousness for they
shall be filled—with the fulness of God!"

Each individual must begin to "hunger and thirst"
for the divine spiritual food which only God, the
Father can bestow. Each must yearn for that individual contact with God for the bringing forth of
that great Light of Truth that he might comprehend all things. This Light has lain dormant, locked
within the rock-hewn sepulcher of man's own being,
because of either the hardness of his heart, or the
easily pacified yearnings of his unawakened soul.

Man himself must begin to desire that Light and
the contact with God with a yearning and a hungering that is so intense it can only be appeased by
partaking of "all righteousness" fully and completely.

When one begins to take upon himself the responsibility of his own spiritual progress then will he
be fed the divine spiritual food of Almighty God
and be clothed in the white raiment of Christ's holy
Light and will be admitted into the Church of the
Firstborn. In this membership he is given a place
and a standing with The Great Brotherhood of Light,
and will forever belong with the heavenly anointed
ones.

Man's divine dominion will be entered when he
has thoroughly established the appetite for divine
or spiritual food in a great "hungering" and then
learned to appease that inner "hungering and thirsting after righteousness" by abiding by the holy, divine laws of righteousness. When one yearns or desires to actually KNOW God for himself and seeks
Him both early and diligently, he will find HIM.
Such is the eternal promise of God.

And as this great "hungering and thirsting after
righteousness" is developed one will never again be
satisfied with an unmanly diet of milk. But, like
Paul of old, he will demand to go beyond the first
principles of the Gospel, of faith and repentance
and baptism and the laying on of hands. He will,
of necessity go on to fulfill all the laws of perfection.
This alone is righteousness. And these higher laws
are the only ones that can prepare one to enter into
membership with God's holy sons of Light.

The divine laws of God's Kingdom are given in
such a way that none can use them who do not comprehend their value and who have not learned to

apply them "righteously." One must grow into them even as a child must grow into usefulness and maturity else its life will be wasted and in vain. And righteousness is the true reality of Godliness. Self-righteousness is but the deceptive childishness of makebelieve.

These wondrous laws of loving God and of seeking for Him diligently are the laws that must be lived by all who would attain unto membership in the "General Assembly and Church of the First-born," or be admitted into the "Great Brotherhood of Light."

Any individual who will but believe or *be* and *live* according to these higher standards and who will continue to "hunger and thirst" for the power to fulfill them, will grow into all truth and comprehend all things. And all things will eventually become subject unto him "both in heaven and on earth." This is the power and the reality of membership in the Church of the First-born. And he who continues "to hunger and thirst after righteousness will be filled—with the fulness of God" and with His divine power.

None of the churches of this earth have contained these inner laws, nor have they revealed the way of their fulfilling. The worldly, secular laws of the earth deal entirely with the cleansing of the outside of the cup or platter, and are most beautiful in as far as they go. All the mortal churches are organized and set up to take care of the temporal, social and physical salvation of man. But none go on to fulfill the dynamic spiritual laws of perfection.

The Kingdom of Christ, which is not of this world, is the Kingdom of heaven, which is found deep within man. It is the Kingdom of righteousness. And those who seek for it will have all things added unto them. This righteousness cleanses not only the outside of the cup but the inside is hallowed and perfected as well. And every gift, every power, every point of attainment Christ holds out is for all to partake of—FREELY—if they will only fulfill the laws pertaining thereto.

The Church of the Firstborn is a heavenly organization which deals entirely with those holy laws of one's spiritual progress and attainment as one grows into the full measure of himself.

This higher Church, which is not of this world, contains the true laws of *His Kingdom—of heaven*. When it is sought for and its Righteousness fulfilled one will be filled with Light and comprehend all things and will be given all power. This alone is the way of the divine Christ Light. This is the Way of Power. It is the Straight and Narrow Way—The Way Christ traveled. It is the divine, inner way of purification and of fulfilment.

This kingdom is entered through the divine devotion of released, infinite praise, divine love and with increasing thankfulness. It is the Pathway of gracious, compassionate "forgiveness" as one forgives, with infinite mercy all those who have ever trespassed against him. It is the pathway of love,

so divine, so filled with understanding it can behold
no faults or failings and therefore loses the power
to condemn.

It is frequently true, that in traveling this great,
"narrow way of inner accomplishment, one is not
only required to fulfill the law of the angels, it often
demands that "one right wrongs he has never committed," even as Christ took upon Himself the burden
of our errors and our mistakes and our transgressions.

This inner Way is the Pathway of attainment. It
is the Way of eternal, unlimited power and of everlasting glory. It is the Way of the Lord.

This is the way in which one leaves his mortal
heritage behind as he outgrows the infant estate of
his childhood nursery, its nursery rhymes and its
immature little games of "make-believe."

As one rises from his outgrown bed, casting aside
his insufficient covering he will receive the power
to behold and to KNOW God, not *just know about
Him*. He will never again return to the lacks and
the bondage of mortal living. He will receive "The
Life more abundant" and then go on to receive
the great "gift of life eternal" in which he need not
die by relinquishing his precious gift of living life
to the angel of Death. This LIFE is the gift which
Christ came to bestow upon all who would accept
it, and every teaching of His proclaims it and promises it to all those who would only *believe*. And
then to prove His point He added, "If you love me
was for this purpose Christ came. And for this
you will keep my commandments," or sayings. It

purpose He laid down His life and took it up again.

These laws of perfection and love and sublime beauty are the keys of His Kingdom, and the laws pertaining to it. And this is the Pathway of His glory.

As one lives the inner laws of righteousness, his own voice of conscience, or inner contact with God will become more and more acute in its direction. Soon that voice becomes a loving voice of tender, revealing glory and complete unfolding, until all the laws of righteousness are fully comprehended. This voice of conscience is the voice of God. As one learns to heed it he will find that divine contact and will eventually be filled with Light and comprehend all things. In this condition no power in existence can restrict that individual from entering into "that membership with the Great Brotherhood of Light." Such a one will be given all power and thenceforth he will belong to "The Assembly of the Living God! This is the Kingdom that is not laws, *will no longer be under the law*," as John so faithfully proclaimed. As he is released from the "outside law" of his childish existence he will receive the fulfillment of every promise and every blessing—and every power.

This is the divine Kingdom of Jesus Christ, Son of the Firstborn," for he, "having fulfilled all the of this world!" That inner song of praise and love and gratitude releases one's own powers of glory in a vibrancy of increasing, radiant splendor from right within himself as it fulfills the law of love. It is the state in which "one's mind and lips lose the power to hurt and wound." It is the stage of advancement when one no longer condemns another for what he does not do. He ceases to be an "accuser," even in his thoughts. In losing the power to condemn or accuse or to find fault he is freed from every hold of evil and every inclination to become "a devil!"

These laws of perfection are the laws Christ unfolded and few there are who have followed that Straight and Narrow Way. His Path contains the laws of loving, or giving and of forgiving; the laws of devotion and a willingness to go the second mile; to give one's cloak to him who has already demanded more than he was entitled to; to share continually; to hold no resentments or vibrations of retaliation. His law contains the admonition to love God with every cell and fiber and sinew, and with all one's strength. His law demands that one's love for his neighbor be as great as his love for himself, if not greater.

The laws Christ gave are so pure, so perfect, so sublime, nothing evil can remain in the individual who undertakes to fulfill them, or to travel that breathtaking "road of holiness." His law requires that one worships and adores and rejoices in every circumstance and under every condition, even the most adverse and distressing. Then it is that one proves his love. And then it is that one will so have proved his love all things will begin to work together for his good—"and the evils of his life will be overcome." This is the only possible way of overcoming evil.

These are the laws of Righteousness, the laws pertaining to His Kingdom, the eternal, irrevocable laws of divine perfection, the supreme, glorious way of fulfilling, without strife or confusion or self-righteous or impossible strivings. It is all fulfilled in just LIVING the laws. Then comes the KNOWING, and "knowledge is power!"

"Live the laws and you will know of their truth" and of their power. "And anything you ask in His Name, or in that divine vibration of His released Light, will be given unto you!" "You can ask anything in that vibration of singing glory, which is His Light, and it will be granted unto you." You will have the power to do the works which He did—even greater works. And you will become "A member in the Great Brotherhood of Light!"

These are the promises of Almighty God to all men, if they will only LIVE the laws pertaining thereto. These laws cannot fail, "neither can these promises return unto Him void and unfulfilled." These higher laws are the same from all eternity to all eternity, for they are the everlasting laws of His Eternal Kingdom. They are irrevocable! "For if you obtain any blessing from God it is by obedience to that law upon which it is predicated." "If you do as I say, then am I bound!" These are the laws of all-power. And they are your own from now on, henceforth, and forever—to fulfill or to ignore and reject.

These sacred laws contain the complete revelation or unfolding of "the most sacred, inner doctrine" known of old. They have been held in secret down the ages. It was forbidden to divulge them, except to those who, through years of preparation, proved themselves worthy to receive. The neophytes or holy scholars of olden times were initiated into these most divine truths, after years of preparation. As they progressed in the use of the higher laws and powers they were known as "adepts" even as they became adept in using the laws rightly or in "righteousness."

These higher laws of His Kingdom were also taught, under the direct injunction of God, to the most spiritual ones of the ancient School of the Prophets. But these most holy teachings were only imparted orally to those whom God selected to receive. They were considered to be far too sacred to be given to the masses lest they trample them under their feet.

So it was that only to the prepared initiates were these divine, holy laws of power revealed. Never before in the history of the world have these sacred rules been written down in plain and simple language. They have been veiled in parables and in figurative phrases. This is the first time they have been written and sent out to the world—"THAT ALL MEN MIGHT BE LEFT WITHOUT EX-CUSE!" These are "the great and mighty truths that have been hid up from the foundation of the world because of the great wickedness of unbelief."

The fulfilling of these divine laws of righteousness

contain the complete instructions of admittance into "the Church of the Firstborn," and the method of becoming a member among the "Priests and Priestesses of Golden Radiance!"

I have been commanded to write these words of Almighty God that not only all men might be left without excuse, but that all who desire might understand and begin to fulfill the higher teachings of "righteousness," that they might partake of the limitless power they embrace.

From the least to the greatest, all are now invited to come and partake of the feast of the King's Son. From the highways and the byways they are summoned to the spiritual banquet, "that God might perform His work, His strange work: and bring to pass His act, His strange act; that all men might be left without excuse. And that all men might judge between the righteous and the wicked, saith your God!"

THE RECORD OF MY TRIAL AND
OF MY LOVE

Chapter XII

After Reason and I had kneeled in our Gethsemane, and after the mockery of the trial, which
had pronounced me a heretic and an out-cast on
the earth, we were sent forth to wander, according
to the hope and the belief of those who had passed
judgment upon me, into eternal darkness forever.
They believed that their decision would send me
into the nethermost depths of the bottomless pit to
wreathe in anguish and remorse.

And the modern Saul of Tarsus, who was prose-
cutor, jury and judge at that trial, insisted the work
was false because "I was an obscure person." So
many times was the phrase, *"You,* an obscure person," repeated I lost track of the number. It was
held forth in deriding reproach and mockery. And

only in the utterance of those words did I find any comfort.

Christ had been condemned as *"an obscure person,"* the son of a carpenter. "The Maid of Orleans, Joan of Arc, was burned at the stake because she was from an *obscure* family and an *obscure* village. Another prophet was condemned and martyred because he claimed to have received a revelation from God and testified that he had seen an angel. And again, those in high places shouted down his testimony, mocked and persecuted him and finally martyred him because he was an *obscure* boy, the son of a farmer.

In my veins ran the blood of martyrs and of kings and of nobles and of pilgrims and pioneers. My heritage was not obscure, but I was not the one to boast of it. It was enough that I could lay claim to being a daughter of God, and know fully that it was so.

I could have taken my accuser into any court in the land and left him standing naked and abashed. I could have sued him and the church he represented for many thousands of dollars—and collected. But he was as sincere in his fanaticism as was Saul of Tarsus, if not as truthful. And I had nothing against the man except a deep regret and an eternal sorrow for his blindness.

So I did not take my case, for appeal, to any judge or jury on this earth. I took my case to the highest authority in existence and at the feet of my Father I knelt. And at His hands I received my comfort. And the Holy Spirit of Promise bore witness to my soul of great and mighty things to come.

So it was in the title of *"obscurity"* I found a measure of solace. I had laid no claim to greatness. Neither did I ask for credits nor for rewards, nor for followers. I wrote because God had commanded me to write, and because this work had been assigned to me before ever I came to earth.

I wrote His words down to the best of my ability and in turn delivered them into the hands of others and they will be held accountable for their distribution. And to each of you who read them is delegated and assigned a portion of the responsibility of sharing this work with others.

It must be here understood that these books were not written to gather together into groups the believers. Rather was this work sent forth to gather up the *unbelievers*.

And so it is.

There have been no churches or creeds or groups to advertise or push forward these books. The publishers have made no extra effort to fulfill their part of the assignment. And no individual has been called to stand at the head of this work or to form an organization to promulgate the teachings of perfection—or to convert others to them.

For, as the writer of the Odes of Solomon proclaimed in his twenty-third Ode: "And there was seen at its head, the head which was revealed even

the Son of Truth from the Most High Father."
(Lost Books of the Bible).

This twenty-third Ode, concerning a sealed docu-
ment, which has so puzzled the scholars and trans-
lators, is the revelation concerning this work. And
I was taught the full meaning of this chapter before
ever I came to earth.

Again, part of this particular Ode must be given
here that an explanation of its meaning might be
comprehended. It is as follows:

"His (God's) thought was like a letter; His will
descended from on high, and it was sent like an
arrow which is violently shot from the bow;

"And many hands rushed to the letter to seize it
and to take it and read it:

"And it escaped their fingers and they were af-
frighted at it and at the seal that was upon it.

"Because it was not permitted to them to loose its
seal: for the power that was over the seal was
greater than they.

"But those who saw it went after the letter that
they might know where it would alight, and who
should read it and who should hear it." (The fore-
going is most assuredly true. Those who went after
the letter, or book, set up a gestapo spying system
to find out who had copies of the book and each
was threatened with excommunication unless they
rejected them or promised to remain silent concerning them).

Now, to continue: "But a wheel (which is a movement of the power of God) received it and came over it.

"And there was with it a sign of the Kingdom and of the Government:

"And everything which tried to move the wheel it moved and cut down:

"And *it gathered the multitude of adversaries,* and bridged the rivers and crossed over and rooted up many forests and made a broad path.

"The head went down to the feet, for down to the feet ran the wheel, and that which was a sign upon it.

"The letter was one of command, for there were included in it all districts: (mental, physical and spiritual as well as the past, the present and the future);

"And there was seen at its head, the head which was revealed even the Son of Truth from the Most High Father.

"And He inherited and took possession of everything. And the thought of many was brought to nought.

"And *all the apostates hasted and fled away, And those who persecuted and were enraged became extinct.*

"And the letter was a great volume which was wholly written by the finger of God."

Such was the ancient proclamation concerning this work and its coming forth. And I was taught this Ode and told the meaning of it before ever I was born. I was so thoroughly instructed in its full interpretation I was almost overcome when it came again into my hands in this life. It was placed in my hands, by the power of God, as I was typing the volume "Ye Are Gods."

Now, to explain the verse concerning the movement, or wheel, which was to receive this work. It is breathtakingly beautiful! As before stated, no advertising or group or church or organization has pushed this work forward, yet each book has continued to be reprinted, according to the demands of those who have asked for or requested copies.

This movement is a movement of love, the dynamic love of God as it shed forth through the hearts of the children of those who read, with love. To you inspired ones, who have read and loved this work, has come the divine desire to share it with your beloved ones, your friends and acquaintances. And so they have continued to go out in an ever-widening circle of increasing participation and of sharing.

And for each of you noble ones, who have shared this work with others, there is a record kept and the angels have rejoiced and are rejoicing over you. You are the true "minister of this sacred draught" of the waters of life as recorded in the sixth Ode, commencing with the sixth verse, which is as follows:

"And the praise of His name He gave us: our spirits praise His Holy Spirit.

"For there went forth a stream and became a river great and broad:" (In verse one of the 39th

Ode is given this definition of great rivers: "Great rivers are the power of the Lord. And they carry headlong those who despise Him: and entangle their paths").

Again, to continue with the sixth Ode:

"For it (the river) flooded and broke up everything and it brought (water) to the Temple:

"And *the restrainers of the children of men were not able to restrain it, nor the arts of those whose business it is to* restrain waters:

"For it spread over the whole earth, and filled everything: and all the *thirsty* upon earth were given to drink of it:

"And *thirst* was relieved and quenched: for from the Most High the draught was given.

"*Blessed then are the ministers of that draught* who are entrusted with that water of His:

"They have assuaged the dry lips, and the will that had fainted they have raised up;

"And souls that were near departing they have caught back from death:

"And limbs that had fallen they straightened and set up:

"They gave strength for their feebleness and light to their eyes:

"For everyone knew them in the Lord, and they lived by the waters of life forever, Hallelujah!"

After one learns of the powers of God and the great glory of His laws and commandments mere mortal living becomes an ugly, drab, unattractive condition. In the dreariness of discords and negation

it becomes impossible to anyone who has learned to
"lift his eyes to the glory of God." It is when one
learns to "hold his eyes single to that glory that he
reaches the degree of understanding in which his
whole being and soul demands that he reach through
the veil of darkness into a higher way of existence.
His "hungering and thirsting after righteouness"
becomes so intense he has to find the bread and
water of life or perish. This "hungering and thirsting" is the need to actually KNOW God. This is
a natural developing, progressive, purifying experience that must be fulfilled. It is the divine
"draught" of the pure waters sent to all those who
thirst.

The path Christ trod, which so few enter, is the
pathway of perfection as every blessed, glorious law
and teaching He revealed stands out in gleaming
way-marks along that divine and holy path. Every
teaching and every law He gave is but a part of
that path of infinite glory, which ends with the injunction, "Be ye perfect, even as your Father in
heaven is perfect!"

So few have found that path because they have
not "lifted their eyes to behold His glory." And fewer
still have been willing to begin to unload the great
burden of their own weaknesses, their dislikes, their
jealousies and greeds and lusts and pride that the
great fountain of God's love might be opened up
within their hearts. Few have followed the admonition to love God with all their hearts, minds, souls
and strength.

But there are many who become so in love with their own little, fanatical paths of self-righteousness or creeded conformity they by-pass entirely His glorious way of achievement. Some, in their fanatic desire *to be first,* exclude all others from any claim upon God's great mercy, thus disclaiming His divine Fatherhood. They forget that He makes the rain fall on the just and the unjust; the sun to shine on the righteous and the unrighteous as His divine love and understanding enfolds the immensity of all His creations.

And so the way of Christ, the path He trod and left the map for, is by-passed as each travels his own selected road, according to the creed or beliefs he has opened his mind to accept. Some drift in contented, self-satisfied indolence and think they are following Him. Others travel their highway of life in defiant rebellion. Some journey along life's road with nothing but vanity and pride, others in self-righteousness, cruel bigotry, for bigotry is always cruel in its blindness and intolerance. And none of these have ever found the Path, nor stepped one foot upon it.

Yet the Path Christ trod is so easy and so beautiful. It is the pathway of love and mercy and compassion and infinite understanding and divine, holy forgiveness held out in a selfless service. There will be another chapter revealing the complete keys to His Way.

And then it was that I, who love Christ above all others, was acclaimed to be the great anti-Christ, to justify the mockery of my excommunication. And surely such a shameful, terrifying accusation would of itself hurl me out of "obscurity," though those who so hopefully proclaimed me such did not realize it.

How could that blessed man, who was a brother I had known and admired in a pre-existent world, in the zeal of his position, possibly know of my love for God and for His Beloved Son, Jesus Christ? For in his mortal pride he had closed the doors of his understanding. And I turned my head to hide my sorrow and my tears and the despair of my soul at his great error. For he understood not one of the great and mighty truths which God had commanded me to write. He misquoted the things I had stated. He placed irrelevant words together in meaningless, contradictory ways to make the entire work sound ridiculous. And those who were called to be witnesses believed him because he was one of the high authorities and none of them had ever before seen me, nor known me, nor read the book.

So how could those, who were called to be witnesses at that trial, possibly know the truth? They sat in awed, reverent silence, at what they considered to be a great honor just to be in the presence of so great a man. How could they possibly know the truth concerning me or my work? They were told to look upon me as a sinner. And because they were thus instructed they fulfilled it to the very letter.

There was not one friendly thought or one understanding gleam in any of their eyes or hearts. And

I wondered, in heartbreak, how a record that reasoned, with the power of God, for men to cast aside their faults and failings and strive to become perfect, "even as the Father in heaven is perfect," could be pronounced wicked. Or how a book that proclaimed only the love and the promises of Jesus Christ could possibly be condemned.

Those witnesses did not know it, but they were there for the sole purpose of being witnesses to a great outrage against justice. And some day they will have to acknowledge the purpose of their presence at that trial. It was for a divine purpose, but a far different one from that which they realized. They were not honored. They will be greatly dishonored for having approved of such an outrageous proceding.

These men could not possibly know of my love for God and for His Beloved Son, Jesus Christ. Not one of them had ever before laid eyes upon me. None of them, not even the great *accuser* had ever seen me or spoken one word to me in my life. They were intelligent men, yet not one of them, under the stress of their own pride, considered for a moment that that trial was a mockery to all the forms of justice that had ever existed upon the earth. It was but a "kangaroo Court." I was reiused counsel. My efforts to bear witness to what I had written, or even to defend myself were denied and silenced.

Of what value is any trial when only the prosecution is permitted to bring its unsubstantiated evidence to the hearing?

Only Sally Franchow, a most dearly beloved and noble woman, who had accompanied me there tried to defend me, in vain. For her courageous efforts she too was excommunicated. And my heart broke. Such an affront to justice as a witness for a defendant being condemned also, just for seeking to testify, was never before heard of in American history.

Joan of Arc's trial lasted many days to bear witness of a great injustice. She was questioned many times, and her answers were heard. I was asked no questions. My trial lasted only a few minutes and will also stand for ages as a witness against great wickedness in "high places." I was given only one alternative, and that was to deny the work which God had placed in my hands. And though all the tortures of life and eternity were placed upon me I could not do that. God had commanded me to write, and I had written as He had directed.

My blessed accuser was like Cotton Mather, the Puritan leader of Salem, who appointed himself to be the sword of the Almighty, assuming in his devotion, that he was the wrath of God. And in his mis-directed zeal that early leader put more people to death than he saved by all his preaching.

My eighth great-grandmother, Martha Allen Carrier, was one of those whom he hanged as a witch. He coerced and tortured her children into declaring her such, along with those hysterical, adolescent girls of that day. My seventh great-grandfather, a small child at the time, along with a brother and sister had their hands and feet tied together behind them and were hung up to an old hitching rack.

"This will not hurt you in the least if your mother is a good woman, BUT *if she is a witch* it will be *she* who is torturing you. Remember, only if your mother *is* a witch will you feel any pain or discomfort," and smiling like the Devil himself, the representative of truth slipped away, leaving them to wreathe in agony.

When finally the children were screaming in pain and one had become unconscious, Mather took the settlers down to listen, and to bear witness of that testimony.

"Is your mother a witch?" questioned the spiritual leader of Salem.

"Yes," sobbed the children through the blood that was streaming through their noses and mouths.

The unconscious child was revived and in a dazed agony answered that awesome question, without realizing what it meant. In a gasping, weak little affirmative he mumbled, "Yes."

Physical violence was not used in this great modern day. The tactics were far more subtle. There was flattery and some very casual bribery and a little falsehood made to look very white, and a secret, gestapo method used to silence those who openly declared their delight in that first book. And like those of Christ's day, the individuals without too much courage, denied their belief in truth lest they be cast out of the synagogue, which, like in days of old, was considered the greatest catastrophe of all.

Still, not sure of her guilt, Martha Carrier, at her trial, was offered her life if she would confess she was a witch. And Martha Carrier stood up straight and tall and answered, "I would rather hang any day than say I was anything as horrible as a witch!"

And so she was hung.

And thus, great men, in the zeal of their calling have sometimes desecrated the positions they have held.

I was offered continued membership in a church that had already, even before my trial, sent out word that I had been cast out and disowned. How those statements could have been recalled had I proclaimed that I was a liar and had been deceived by Satan, and that God never commanded me to write His words, I do not know.

But then, such promises had been offered to others, before me, and they had complied with the seemingly righteous request of the leaders only to be humiliated and cast out with their own confessions standing against them. I did not know this until later. But under no consideration could I turn against God and defile His work and debauch Him by denying His power.

I was not hanged as a witch. I was not crucified. I was stoned to death. And the great man who hurled those stones of mockery and falsehood had others hold his cloak while he did the stoning. And those stones were very deadly in the hands of a man so great.

In the tragedy of my heartbreak and in the overwhelming grief of my sorrow, for that man had robbed me of everything my life had consisted of, I went forth an outcast. I went to the mountains to cry out my anguish in tears as I buried my face in the dust and wept in the despairing agony of my soul.

And an angel of the Lord came to me and I was given direction to cover that period of my life —and was taken away that they saw me not again for three years, then only for so short a period I was gone before they realized I had been there.

And they rejoiced as they lifted up the ancient chant until the valleys echoed with it and the mountains vibrated with the repetition of its tones. And that ancient chant gathered up momentum as the words issued forth: " 'All is well in Zion; Yea, Zion prospereth, all is well!' . . . And thus the devil cheateth their souls, and leadeth them away carefully down to hell." Yes, "Woe unto them that turneth aside the just for a thing of naught and revile against that which is good, and say that it is of no worth! For the day shall come that the Lord God will speedily visit the inhabitants of the earth; and in that day that they are fully ripe in iniquity they shall perish . . . For behold, at that day shall the Devil rage in the hearts of the children of men, and stir them up to anger against that which is good. And others will he pacify and lull them away into carnal security."

"Therefore, woe be unto him that crieth: all is well!

"Yea, woe be unto him that harkeneth unto the precepts of men, and denieth the power of God, and the gift of the Holy Ghost!

"Yea, woe be unto him that saith: We have received, and we need no more!

"And in fine, woe unto all those who tremble, and are angry because of the truth of God! For behold, he that is built upon the rock receiveth it with gladness; and he that is built upon a sandy foundation trembleth lest he shall fall." (Those who are built upon the foundation of pride and self-righteous arrogance tremble in dismay at the thought or idea of perfection, knowing they cannot fulfill it without humbling themselves).

"Woe be unto him that shall say: We have received the word of God, and we need no more of the word of God, for we have enough!

"For behold, thus saith the Lord God: I will give unto the children of men line upon line, precept upon precept, here a little and there a little: and blessed are those who hearken unto my precepts, and lend an ear unto my counsel, for they shall learn wisdom; for unto him that receiveth I will give more!" (2 Nephi 28).

That which will be added in abundance is revealed in the following: "And now, behold this is wisdom; whoso readeth, let him understand and receive also: For unto him that receiveth it shall be given more abundantly, EVEN POWER." (D. & C. 71:5-6).

Returning to the first reference, this is given: "From them that shall say, we have enough, from them shall be taken away even that which they have.

"Cursed is he that putteth his trust in man, or maketh flesh his arm, or shall hearken unto the precepts of men, save their precepts shall be given by the power of the Holy Ghost."

So declared an ancient prophet centuries ago. And the prophecy stands and is being fulfilled at the present time. And I, Annalee Skarin, am called to bear witness of it. And this record is my witness. And the seal of God is upon it.

And now, I am instructed to proclaim my great love and to make it known that the whole world might worship and adore the great Almighty God, Creator of heaven and of earth, and His Beloved Son, Jesus Christ.

I stand completely humbled as I am commanded to bear the fullness of my testimony and reveal the power of my love that some of the false rumors that have been circulated concerning me, by those without knowledge or understanding, might be silenced.

The record goes back a long way, back to the ending of twenty-one years of unfortunate, unhappy marriage. It goes back to the time when God released me from those bonds, according to a promise He had made to me years before. I was taken away and released from that marriage after I had been betrayed and cheated and my progress completely stopped and my field of service closed and all chances of fulfilling my destiny were barred.

It is also necessary to explain here just how and why I had learned to hear God when He spoke. My life had been filled with heartaches and wants and tragedy and suffering from childhood and I could not have survived if I had not learned to go to God for comfort and for help and for instruction. In my early childhood I had learned the power of prayer. And God never failed me. Sometimes His answers did not come in the way I desired them, but always they came in His own way and according to His own wisdom, which continually proved to be far greater than mine. And in time I learned to listen, though at first, I often argued with the information or instructions He gave. Eventually I learned to not only heed—but to KNOW.

And so this record goes back to the time when Reason, whom I had loved across a continent and twenty-three years, was sent by God, to take me away.

Reason and I had loved each other before ever the world began. And before the mountains were formed or the rivers ran God had tied the bonds of an eternal union. And God Himself reaffirmed that union after we were brought together again.

In this life a continent had separated us for twenty-three years. And I had lived with him in my heart and he had lived with a small picture of me upon his dresser. And in those years before, when first we met, the forces of darkness, knowing the future of our work, placed a hundred wedges between us and our broken hearts. And in that time of tragic sorrow we had each made the pledge to the other to live as nearly perfect as we could—all the days of our lives. We shook hands on it at our last farewell. And no one knew of the anguish of that parting nor of our heartbreak and our tears for such love as ours few could understand for few have ever known.

Then, after many years, when all things had failed and the time of testing and of our developing into a knowledge of the full meaning of life, God took a hand to fulfill His promises and brought us together again.

And in our love for God, and for His Beloved Son, we renewed our pledge to live as nearly perfect as we could — to intentionally or knowingly break no law or commandment, but to strive to fulfill each and every injunction ever uttered by God. We pledged ourselves to serve only Him all the days of our lives. We covenanted to live in virtue, abstaining from sexual intercourse, that we might not be guilty of transgressing any of the divine, higher laws. And since I had been married, and was divorced this seemed a most necessary pledge to us. Christ's injunction concerning divorce and re-marriage being considered adulterous on the higher level, we could take no other course than to make a covenant of complete abstinence.

It was easy to make the pledge for our souls were willing—but our flesh was weak. Our love was very great. The joy of being together, after so many years, was in itself stupendously dynamic. God said, "I give men weaknesses that they might be strong!" It is surely not the weaknesses that give men strength but in the overcoming of those weaknesses.

We would spend half our nights upon our knees pleading with God to give us power to fulfill our covenant and to sanctify our lives in virtue, unto Him. And in the effort we exerted we had a small hope that our terrific struggle would help atone for some of the adulterous wickedness of this generation.

And only Reason and I and God and His angels, know of the fires of that testing. If we had been married many years, or even several years it would not have been so difficult. But we were newly wed— and we were in love. I loved him with every singing, vibrating cell of my body. I loved him with all my heart. I loved him with my mind and with all my intelligence. And our bodies were young and strong, for they had not aged in the years. And we were mortal. We did not then realize that we were already striving for immortality. Perhaps it would have been easier had we known.

Very humbly we were seeking to serve God with all our strength—then with all our hearts and minds and souls. And where our strength was weak God gave us power to subdue our flesh. And after a year the fires of our crucifixion were in complete control. And the problem of sex was taken entirely from our lives and all the desires of the flesh. And our love became even greater. Our love was unsullied and unmarred by any physical defilement.

We loved with a pure love that sang and vibrated at each touch, that was held in each glance, that rose in triumphant waves of singing splendor to vibrate across the universe and play new melodies upon the very stars.

Each caress was a sacrament of wonder. Each kiss contained a thrill of glory. Life never became sordid nor drab nor ugly. Nor did we ever take each other for granted.

As Reason would hold me in his arms each cell and fiber of my entire being would vibrate and sing in ecstatic, melodious wonderment, and my whole body would sing in reverberating splendor, "I love you! I love you! I love you!" My heart sang it! My soul sang it and every atom of my being sang it! My blood carried the glory of that love as it coursed through my veins with every pulse-beat. And with every breath that song vibrated on and out and up. And that love has continued to increase. It is a love that is dynamically eternal. It is beautiful beyond description and in a devotion of sanctification it has continued to increase.

And then, as Reason would hold me in his arms, our love would blend and go on out in adoring glory to the very throne of God and all the heavens and the earth were included in it. Our hearts would open as wide as eternity in a melting glory of unspeakable, reverent, holy devotion. Our love, of itself, would

go out to place its tribute of tenderness and sanctified, rapturous fervor at God's very throne.

Then, increasing, that love would vibrate out to
enfold the world and every living soul upon it in an
holy anointment of healing.

In the sharing of this sacred information I am not
saying that abstinence from sex is the fulfilment of
the full law of righteousness. I am saying that *the
deep love we held for God,* and *the willingness to
obey His* EVERY *injunction and command* fulfilled
the law of His righteousness.

The very power to condemn or to judge was lost
and overcome in the greatness of our love. And here
I must add, I hold no thought of dislike or resentment against those who were the instigators and the
executors at my trial. It is only told here because I
have been instructed to make a record of it. And I
have done so without resentment or a desire to re-
taliate.

I am instructed to write these facts for a very
definite reason. God has informed me that those who
continue to fight against me and this work will be
taken from the earth if necessary, to silence them.
Or as the writer of the Odes of Solomon declared,
concerning this work: "And all those who persecuted and were enraged became extinct!" I have
pleaded with God to bless all who read these books
and to soften their hearts that they might not revile
against His work. At first I earnestly offered myself
that those who did condemn or fight against it might
be spared that they would not be destroyed or perish

from the earth. Such is my love. And my forgiveness is complete. I gladly offered not only my life but my soul that those who would reject His words might be forgiven.

Such is the love God has placed in our hearts. It is the pure, Christ-like love which God sheds forth through the hearts of those who love Him, and keep His commandments. It is a love that enfolds the whole world and all who live upon it—and all who have ever lived or who will live upon it in the future. It is a love that is more powerful than all the hates and prejudices and discords in existence. It is a love that knows no fear. It is a love of mercy and compassion and forgiveness. *It is the love of God!*

It is the love that has dispelled and conquered all physical weariness. It has banished negation. It has eliminated pain and affliction. IT HAS CON-QUERED DEATH!

Such has been our love for God and for the divine teachings of His Beloved Son, Jesus Christ! And such has been the return of the love God has shed forth through our hearts. All physical mortal claims lost their hold and we were lifted beyond the human demands of the flesh into a condition of utter glory, of continual joy and ever increasing splendor as new fields of service opened before us in an ever upward, progressing of eternal wonder.

We were lifted into a world where sorrow is not and where pain and sin are unknown.

It is a dimension where vibrations are the reality. And in this higher realm there is no pretentions for vibrations can not be faked or assumed or pretended. Vibrations are the cause behind the effects. The effects are only the outward show or the manifestation of the results which vibrations establish.

In this sphere all pride, negation, jealousies, greeds and lusts along with the hates and dislikes are forgotten and left behind.

This is not a realm in which none ever knew or ever had weaknesses or committed sins. This is the world inhabited by those who *"overcame"* their weaknesses, "while in the flesh." It is the world where "mortals have evolved from the man kingdom into the God Kingdom" by stupendous effort and ever increasing love. It is the realm inhabited by "just men made perfect" through their own desiring and striving and hope as it becomes KNOWING.

This realm holds forth to all who can only *believe* and attain thereto, by following the path Christ marked, the way of continual, divine spiritual progress along the holy highway of "overcoming."

This realm is where Christ rules. It is the Kingdom of the Firstborn. And its gates are opened wide to all. It is the great spiritual Zion, the reward of the pure in heart. The way to this glorified City of Righteousness is so plainly marked and so simple a fool need not err therein, though the wicked can never cross over, as Isaiah proclaimed. The way is the Path Christ trod, the way of love and compassion and divine obedience to every law in the divine *overcoming* and the conquering of death, which is but the seal of Satan, author of death. It is the path of prayer.

In this realm there are various grades and districts. And they are all glorious beyond man's comprehension, for (human) "eye hath not seen, neither hath it entered into the heart of man the great things which God has prepared for those who love Him."

It is not possible to share more of these divine truths with you because they can only be expressed further in a language which is entirely spiritual. It is the language of truth—the language of pure vibration. Lift your vibrations through love and prayer and the bringing forth of the Divine Christ Light within you and you will comprehend the language, for then you will fulfill all the laws pertaining to the Kingdom of Righteousness. Then you will need none to teach you for God Himself will be your teacher.

"A PILLAR IN THE TEMPLE OF GOD!"

Chapter XIII

There are repetitions in this work but each time a truth or passage of scripture is repeated new information is unfolded. The nine digits and the zero are repeated in every mathematical problem of arithmetic, yet each problem is different.

If some of the phrases of wisdom and promise are repeated again know that a new and advanced bit of information is being opened to reveal more clearly the glorious pathway of Light—The Path He trod.

In Isaiah, chapter forty, verses twenty-eight to thirty-one, is given this divine information: "Hast thou not known? Hast thou not heard, that the everlasting God, the Lord, the Creator of the ends of the earth, fainteth not, neither is weary? There is no searching his understanding . . . He giveth power to the faint; and to them that hath no might he increaseth strength; . . . Even the youths shall faint and be weary, and the young men shall utterly fall. But they that wait upon the Lord shall renew their strength; they shall mount up with wings as eagles; they shall run and not be weary; and they shall walk and not faint."

This divine information and promise that "they shall mount up with wings as eagles" is not an idle promise nor are these sacred words vain and meaningless.

Christ repeated and verified this promise in his conversation with Nicodemus in the record of St. John, chapter three, verses one to eight and verse twelve, as follows: "There was a man of the Pharisees, named Nicodemus, a ruler of the Jews:

"The same came to Jesus by night, and said unto him, Rabbi, we know that thou art a teacher come from God: for no man can do these miracles that thou doest, except God be with him.

"Jesus answered and said unto him, Verily, verily, I say unto thee, Except a man be born again, he cannot see the kingdom of God.

"Nicodemus saith unto him, How can a man be born when he is old? Can he enter the second time into his mother's womb, and be born?

"Jesus answered. Verily, verily, I say unto thee, Except a man be born of the water and of the Spirit, he cannot enter into the Kingdom of God.

"That which is born of the flesh is flesh; and that which is born of the spirit is spirit.

"Marvel not that I said unto thee, ye must be born again.

"The wind bloweth where it listeth, and thou hearest the sound thereof, but *canst tell whence it cometh and whether it goeth*: SO IS EVERY ONE WHO IS BORN OF THE SPIRIT."

Verse twelve: "If I have told you earthly things, and ye believe not, how shall ye believe, if I tell you of heavenly things?"

These books have been written to make that earthly pathway plain and discernible to all who wish to travel it. It is a pathway of utter glory but those who cannot follow even its earthly markers and instructions cannot possibly comprehend the heavenly information. For this reason it cannot be revealed, not that God is not eager to share the most sublime truths of heaven with every child of earth, but they are not prepared to receive them. Only those who begin to apply the sacred, divine teachings Christ left behind will be prepared to enter into and to comprehend the glories of the heavenly realm.

The path is so straight and so narrow it is not wide enough for one to turn around in and go back. Those who enter the path and then cease to travel it will find it is a greased slide going downward toward the Nether Regions, for God will not be mocked. And those who view the splendor of that glorious pathway then return, "like the swine to his wallow, or the dog to his vomit," will the more speedily be destroyed, for they will destroy themselves. However few, who even catch a glimpse of the unutterable glory of His kingdom seldom fail to reach it, It is only those without vision who perish.

The difficulty comes in the effort it takes to find the path, not in the traveling of it.

It is true that as one travels this Inner Way of purification he is required to leave the old, familiar, worldly teachings and orthodoxed conformities behind. But this should cause no regrets for they are musty with age and shabby with use. Even the things which afford a man the greatest pleasures, uncontrolled hilarity, his hidden lusts and weaknesses and the broad open way of secular enjoyments become repulsive and abhorrent as one steps out into the divine pathway of prayer.

Prayer is the path—the prayer of praise and love and singing gratitude. And it becomes increasingly more beautiful as one travels it. Then finally one learns, to his astonishment, that this upward path of glory is not a horizontal road but a perpendicular one. This pathway is the progressive, exalting one of his own ascension.

One is not aware that the path is almost vertical, as he travels it. He only realizes this fact as he nears the completion of his own journey of purification. As he is given the power to take his spiritualized body of flesh and bones, "to come and go without anyone being able to tell where he came from or where he goes" will he realize fully the stupendous powers and breathtaking glory of that divine path. He will realize that the journey along that upward road was the greatest, most rewarding experience possible to have had. In looking back he will know that every living moment of the struggle was a divine achievement of unutterable worth. He will know fully that he has traveled the path Christ indicated and left the map for.

And the life of such a one becomes sanctified and all powers are henceforth his to use in the great assignments into which he will be directed in a divine service of ever increasing, joyous wonder.

In the achievement of this journey of purification one will become "a pillar in the temple of God and will go no more out," for he will have overcome all the ugly, sordid, morbid, evil, dreary things of mortal living.

He will comprehend fully his place and know that a pillar is one of the glorified columns of strength that supports the whole divine structure of that celestial edifice of eternal truth and divine light. He becomes a very part of that empyreal glory as he lends his strength to uphold the entire works of supreme, celestial truth.

In order to travel this straight and narrow path into the divine realms of Light one must learn to "hold his eyes single to that glory, even to the glory of God." It is in vision that one first glimpses the wonders of such beauty as his soul awakes to behold "those things that can become" — not "the things that might have been." In adoration and love one's eyes automatically become single to that celestial glory of God.

To attain to this vision of divine beauty one must go into the center of his own soul, as "he becomes

still." Within that center of himself, the very stillness of his own soul, one will learn to abide within
the vibrating, exulting praise of divine love and
thankfulness and spiritual rejoicing. In this holy,
high vibration, which is the pure Christ Light, no
darkness can abide. In this vibration, as one learns
to hold himself within its divine glow, one is naturally filled with Light. He becomes clothed in this
Light and will begin to comprehend all things. To
such a one God will unveil His face, according to
His divine promise given unto the children of men.
And His promises cannot fail. "If ye do as I say
then am I bound."

The promises and the information concerning this
Path and the glories to which it leads has been there
for centuries just waiting for man to begin to LIVE
the laws He gave that they might KNOW the truth
and the power of God's fulfilment.

"And when thou prayest, thou shalt not be as the
hypocrites are: for they love to pray standing in
the synagogues and in the corners of the streets, that
they may be seen (and heard) of men. Verily I say
unto you, They have their reward. But thou, when
thou prayest, enter into thy closet, and when thou
hast shut thy door, pray to thy Father which is in
secret; and thy Father which seeth in secret shall
reward thee openly. And when ye pray, use not vain
repetitions, as the heathen do: for they think that
they shall be heard for their much speaking."

Within the secret closet of man's self is the place
of prayer, the Holy of Holies, the most Secret Place

of the Most High, the place of the feast of the Pass-
over, or holy sacrament. While abiding within this
holy place of high devotion, one is truly abiding in
God. He is literally clothed in the Light of Christ
and death cannot touch him. As one learns to abide
continually in this Secret Place of the Most High,
he will have the power to overcome death—"and
it will pass him by as the Children of Israel and
not slay him."

And as one releases his prayers from deep within
himself, not just word or lip prayers, but prayers
from the center of his soul, he is traveling that straight
and narrow way. From the very depths of his soul
one must send forth his prayers with real intent. This
is the place of holy communion. It is where one partakes of the bread and waters of life. It is the place
of divine contact with God. And as one learns to
enter this quiet, inner closet of his own soul, he is
"asking in spirit. And he that asketh in spirit asketh according to the will of God and he shall receive whatsoever he asketh." So is the promise of
God. Or as just quoted: "The Father which is in
secret shall reward thee openly." Or bring to pass
the outward fulfilling of thy soul's request.

The pathway of glory, that divine, straight and
narrow way is the pathway of prayer. And this prayer
is the secret, sacred petition of each man's own soul
as he lifts his eyes to behold the great glory of God
and begins to hunger and thirst for those rays of
glory to penetrate his mortal being, that he might
be clothed in their Light. This divine prayer is not

a string of vain repetitions or monotonous mono-
logues. This prayer is the releasing of that divine
Christ Light, through a supreme devotion of everlasting joy as one's eyes become single to the glory
of God and his mortal will begins to take on the holiness of God's divine Will. This prayer is the prayer
of praise and love and gratitude, released from the
soul in that triumphant, glorious New Song of Celestial Creation.

This inner prayer of sacramental feasting, as one
partakes of the bread and waters of life, is established in that praising adoration of eternal, victorious triumph released through the heartstrings of
the soul. As one uses these powers of praise and love
and thanksgiving, the Celestial Cord of eternal glory,
his own life is brought into divine harmony with the
heavenly glories of eternal progress and stupendous,
celestial unfoldment as death is overcome.

As one enters that closet of himself to pray to
God, he must close the door to all outside, worldly
distractions. And then he must hold it closed. As
one practices this he will eventually find that "he
goes no more out!"

This is the path in which one lives his life instead
of permitting his life to live him. This is the pathway of power in which one is no longer pushed and
shoved about by every outside condition, vibration,
circumstance or inclination. Neither does one need
to stand up battling the eternal, nagging conflicts
of a dreary, mortal existence of drudgery or violence.

The path of prayer is the path of power. And in

traveling this divine, inner way of praise and love and gratitude and devotion one is lifted into ever and ever higher realms of glorious light until "he is filled with light and comprehends all things!"

And in your praying, thank God for every blessing you have or do receive. Thank Him for every blessing your neighbors or friends have, or receive, as though those blessings were bestowed personally upon you. Rejoice in the blessings of every living soul, for by envy death came into the world. Pray and give thanks for every blessing of your own and of others. Rejoice and give thanks and jealousy will be forever overcome in you.

"The nearer man approaches perfection the clearer are his views and the greater his enjoyments until he overcomes the evils of his life, and loses every desire for sin; and like the ancients, arrives at the point of faith where he is wrapped in the power and glory of his Maker and is caught up to dwell with Him."

Christ's living, eternal invitation, offered to the world, still stands empty and unanswered: "Come unto me ALL ye who labor." This means literally every child of earth. It is for every mortal soul, for all are laboring to serve mammon in one way or another.

The preachers and ministers may believe they are laboring for God, but without realizing it they are laboring, perhaps even harder than others, for the approval of men and for their financial hire.

Many individuals are only laboring mentally as

they scheme to increase their incomes, their prestige or their popularity. Or they may be laboring for a mere, physical existence of bleakness and hardship.

Yet every individual on the earth who is laboring in any manner or fashion (and all are), are invited to come to Christ. And those who go to Him will be released from the bondage of mammon. Then the rich man will learn that "He is poor and wretched and miserable and blind and naked." The poor man will comprehend his tragic state of affairs fully and realize he has remained in his unhappy condition because of his gross ignorance and his blind unbelief.

Neither the rich man nor the poor man has understood the full desolating condition of his existence and so each has remained in his state of unprogressiveness for a full lifetime, unless he has accepted Christ's holy, loving invitation.

Those who can open their eyes to behold "the glory of God" will comprehend the tragedy of this lone and dreary world, the futility of its emptiness, the drabness of its rewards, the empty bleakness of its recompenses, the impermanence of its compensations. To such "the great hungering and thirsting for a better way, for truth, for righteousness and for release" will become an increasing hunger that will demand appeasement. And for all such there is awaiting "That kingdom of righteousness, where all else will be added" if they will only "ask, seek and knock; for all who ask shall receive and those who seek shall find, and unto those who knock it will be opened."

Now, to complete the promise of Christ's eternal, divine invitation: "Come unto me all ye who labor and are heavy laden and I will give you rest." All who are heavy laden with depts, poverty, sickness, suffering, sorrow or with the burden of their lusts and greeds and hates and prides, or whatever it is that is holding back their progress, He is inviting them to go to Him. Any who become weary with the burdens of life are invited to go to Him. And the eternal promise is awaiting all, "And I will give you rest." He will give you rest from your pain, from your afflictions, from your burdens and from every earthly, mortal tribulation and vicissitude. And to clarify this quotation and enlarge upon it this divine revelation is added: "Which rest is the fulness of my glory!" (D. & C. 84:24).

In the completion of this promise is contained the full invitation of everlasting, dynamic wonder: "Come unto me all you who labor and are heavy laden, and I will give you rest—which rest is the fulness of my glory!" This promise is so dynamically breathtaking none have ever lifted their eyes to behold its unspeakable, wondrous beauty. Nor have any lived it that they might *know* if it is true or not.

His divine promises are all so stupendously glorious none have lifted their vision high enough to behold their true meaning. None have seen their full glory because none have tried to live the laws pertaining to the promises. Man has continued to dwell in the darkness of unbelief. Men have clung to their doubts and their fears and consequently to their evils and misfortunes even while professing His Holy Name. And quite unknowingly they have helped to hold back the great Light as they have blocked its way with the darkness of themselves.

To become a pillar in the temple of God, so that one goes no more out, one must himself become a pillar of Light by traveling that holy, highway of Light. As one becomes a pillar in the temple of God, by overcoming mortality and all its clutching, frustrating claims, one stands forth filled with Light and with power as he lends his strength to support the whole, sublime structure of everlasting, glorious, celestial power and truth. These "pillars" become the upholding supporters of the whole, divine edifice of God. They become one with the Light and the glory.

Lift your eyes to behold His glory! "Hold your eyes single to that glory" as you close the door of mortality and ascend along that "straight and narrow path" into the realms of eternal Light. Leave the dark, muddy road of earth and go to Him, all ye who labor and are heavy laden and receive the fulness of His glory!

This pathway of prayer is not a sanctimonious praying, "to be seen or heard of men." This is the secret, inner way, in which one prays from his heart until that prayer is established in the soul and imprinted upon the very atoms "waiting to become." Then it will be reflected out to glorify and to fulfill and to complete all things, including one's own life. This divine method of prayer becomes a very part of life, in time, as it is practiced in love and joy and thanksgiving. One's life is sanctified as he becomes the prayer, the praise, the glory and eventually the Light. As one establishes that prayer within himself he naturally becomes the prayer of vibrating glory and of eternal Light and is glorified in that Light as he comprehends all things.

Within this power of prayer is released all the burdens of life, all the ills, all the dismays and the evils and one fulfills literally Christ's holy invitation: "Come unto me *all* you who labor, and you who are heavy laden, and I will give you rest—which rest is the fulness of my glory!" And one goes to him by traveling that holy pathway of his own ascension, that "straight and narrow way of overcoming."

It is utterly impossible to keep praying, until every thought and every breath becomes a prayer and not get there. This road of prayer is the pathway of glory—the Path He trod—the secret, inner way of holiness and fulfilment—the Way of God!

This is the reason no man can possibly travel the road for another. It is each individual's own pathway and each must travel his own secret, inner path of purification and fulfilment. This is the Path Christ trod, "The Straight and Narrow Way, which so few find."

There are so many, wonderful facts revealed as one travels this pathway of prayer it is impossible to share them all. I can only reveal a few of the breathtaking marvels of this stupendous road of eternal glory.

The journey is long or short according to the individual's desiring. Some can mosey along it for a lifetime. Others will travel it with speed and concentrated power.

When the prayer has reached into the innermost being of a man and becomes an established part of his make-up, when every cell and fiber is brought under the supreme vibration of that praise and love and gratitude, the journey is completed. It is the journey of man as he takes his body with him into the higher realms through an inner purifying glory of singing ecstasy.

The journey only lasts as long as it is necessary to bring every atom and cell into the rhythm of that high, spiritual vibration of Light as it rejoices in the Celestial Song of Creation, releasing it from his own heart and soul, and finally from his entire being.

The time will come, according to prophecy, when those in an advanced state of spiritual understanding "Will pray day and night for deliverance" from every mortal tie and inclination and claim. For such the journey will be speedy and swift indeed.

The pathway of glory is the pathway of discipline. Only under the regime of self-discipline can one become a true disciple. And only as one chooses to discipline himself can he travel this straight and narrow road, which leads to life eternal—not by dying, but by overcoming death.

Along this pathway of prayer, this sacred, inner

way of dynamic, yielding, melting devotion, in which every mortal cell is converted, transmuted and translated into the divine, spiritual excellence, one learns to abide in the great, eternal NOW. One outgrows the past and all the physical, earthly claims. The great, eternal NOW blends into the forever, endless, perfect, powerful and sublime. In the NOW is the fulfilment—and TIME is no longer. One enters eternity and receives the gift of "Life Eternal," which Christ came to give.

Along this divine pathway of progress and perfection there is no room to carry the great burdens of past errors, mistakes and heartbreaks. One learns to unload these heavy burdens of the flesh at the feet of Christ as he fulfills literally that heavenly invitation: "Come unto me all ye who labor and are heaven laden and I will give you rest—which rest is the fulness of my glory!" Take my yoke upon you; for my yoke of love is easy and my burden is Light"—even the great "Christ Light" of eternal glory.

As one travels this path of prayer he soon becomes clothed in the white raiment so that the shame of his mortal weaknesses, bigotries and failures and all the sins of human defilement will never appear. Neither will they come in remembrance before the Lord, and though they were as scarlet they shall become white as snow.

The divine, white raiment is spun out of the pure, divine Christ Light as it is woven upon the loom of prayer. Only in, and by prayer, can one be clothed in His Holy Light, for this Light is the armor of Christ, the seal of protection, the light of glory. No evil can penetrate this robe of white Light. No darkness can destroy it. It is the fulness of His glory. This Light not only clothes the outside in a protecting armor of power and vibrating ecstasy, it clothes the inside as well for every individual cell receives "the life more abundant," which is Christ's eternal gift to those who fulfill the law.

All are invited to travel the pathway of His glory, this divine, inner way of ascension as "man evolves from the man kingdom into the God Kingdom!"

The road is not difficult! It is beautiful beyond description! Every glorious step of it! It is the road of Light, of love, and of singing ecstasy and eternal happiness in which the dismal ugliness of mortality, and the shameful victory of death is fully "overcome!"

Live His laws and you will *Know!* Fulfill the divine admonition of Paul, the apostle, "Prove all things and hold fast to that which is good!"

*(That men ought always to pray: Luke 18 and the command to pray without ceasing: I Thes. 5:17).

THE THINGS THAT ARE TO COME!

Chapter XIV

Reason and I have been sent to many places and upon many assignments. We have been sent, at times, to test the hearts and souls and the goodness and sincerity of individuals and their integrity and trustworthiness. And we have sometimes been sent to assist in helping to open the understandings of those who are prepared to receive help, or who have requested it.

And of those whom we have been sent to contact few have *known* who we were, though some have suspected. And some of those who have learned of our identity have failed temporarily, not through intention, but because they were so eager to inform others of their experiences and of their having been selected or singled out, as they supposed, above others. These blessed, erring ones are still seeking so ardently to exalt that little mortal self they have retarded their own progress. And these, through many tests and many trials, may perhaps in time overcome in a triumphant glory of release. But first they will have the terrific struggle to overcome that little "self" which they have increased with power and magnified in strength through their own pride and because of their weakness to magnify their own importance. A few have even broken their sacred oath of silence and in doing so have boasted in vain.

And there are many, who are fulfilling the glory of their destinies in magnificent splendor and dynamic progress. These are the ones, who, in silent glory of devotion are yielding that strident, little pride-filled, mortal "self" over to God in an utter and complete surrender of highest devotion. These are gradually receiving their "HIGHER"—calling. Or it could be said, "Their calling and election is made sure." They, in the opening of their own hearts, minds and souls to God are prepared to be "filled with the very fulness of God," and with the complete *knowledge* of Him. They have, through high devotion brought forth that divine Light of Jesus Christ from right within themselves.

In Los Angeles is an assortment of all that is— the wickedness and crime and an undercurrent of evil that is awesome in its power. There are also those who are Devil worshippers and they realize it not. There are those as wildly fanatical in their devotion to false gods as were the ancient inhabitants of Cannan in their worship of the sun God

Baal, or to the monster Molech, to whom they fed their children.

There are numerous cults and creeds in that city neath the sun. And no matter how contorted their beliefs, for there is everything from black magic to worshippers of reincarnation, which denies the resurrection and the divine teachings of Jesus Christ. And there are dozens of distorted ideas of Christianity. And each group is most positive that it alone knows truth or has any claim upon it. And no matter how wierd and contorted and false are the doctrines propounded, there are those who give ear and follow.

And above the tumult and the confusion of Babel comes the gentle, powerful voice of Christ, "My sheep hear my voice, and they *know* me and a stranger they will not follow!"

And many of these great and noble ones, who *know* His voice were directed to Los Angeles as definitely and unerringly as was Christine Mercie. And many since have been called away from that area with a new commission resting on their shoulders. There are various centers in America where His chosen ones are being prepared speedily and swiftly for a part in His dynamic work of glory, though not all of them fully realize it yet, perhaps because they have not been openly called or organized into groups. They, however, are being prepared individually. And occasionally they do meet each other and the power of their meetings is felt over the world.

These noble ones are already beginning to outshine the sun, though they know it not. They cannot yet be given that knowledge lest their exalted pride retard their progress. But it is through these that the bonds of righteousness are being established on the earth in order to withstand the great things which are to come.

No two cities are alike in their receptiveness, their desiring or in their evils or in their devotions.

San Francisco is more orthodoxed; more sealed in traditional conformity; more satisfied with things, just as they are.

Sacramento is almost entirely asleep in its contentment. Reason and I were sent there to fulfill a very important and different type of assignment than any previous one. The moment that assignment was completed we were taken away, only to be called back for one brief half-hour, by one who had requested it with all the strength of her soul. And her request was answered, though from that moment on much more will be required of her.

Chicago is a city where evil is conceived and born. New York is a city of darkness and iniquity. Philadelphia, the city of "Brotherly love" is losing the gift of love speedily and in an alarming degree.

There are many cities which are developing what they believe is a condition of smog. Be it here known that the seeming combination of smoke and fog, along with the gasses and fumes of modern industry is not the entire cause of those shrouded cities. There is a deeper cause behind those veils of darkness. It is a condition more menacing than all the fog and fumes arising over those vast, condemned areas.

Reason and I have been sent to many of these great cities as well as to many individuals in various stages of advancement. The more spiritually advanced an individual is the more his eyes behold the light. And each person beholds us according to his own degree of spiritual understanding. And to many we have remained completely out of vision.

We have been sent to many places and on as many varieties of assignments. We have wept with sorrow as we have beheld the great tidal waves of greed sweep away the powerful, holy strength of honest integrity. Where a man is entitled to make a margin of profit nothing less than a hundred or even a thousand percent is now satisfactory.

Politicians sell out their nations and their people for financial gain. They have sold and are selling their own souls for "thirty pieces of silver" and realize it not. There are many, in high places, who are linked together in secret, evil combinations to rob and plunder the treasuries of the departments in which they have been called to serve. The wealth of many nations is thus being confiscated and drained away in misuse. Many betray every trust as they swagger forth defiled and defiling, plundering and robbing in their refined, cultured way of modern hypocracy.

Only a few times, in the history of the world, have men's clutching hands been so filled with greed, their hearts so contaminated with the lust for wealth that they have lost the gift of mercy. And never have men's minds been so set upon gain. And never have morals been so low except in the great nations of the past, which, ripened in iniquity, were destroyed from the face of the earth, or were left to totter down the ages, shorn of their glory.

In the days of the Spanish despoilers their barbaric conquests for gold alone has equaled the greed of this day. And today, five centuries later, the descendants of those cruel ravagers are the most heartless in their grasping methods. They rob the poor and the hungry and leave their pople in a state of destitute suffering and woe. And that distressing cry of misery is arising to the throne of heaven—and it is not unheard.

These grasping, almost inhuman members of society, these politicians and officials, in high places, whose hands are filled with unlawful gains, are themselves releasing the winds of retribution upon the earth.

Riding those winds is their own destruction as the waves of fury are lashed into a frenzy of overwhelming disaster, for riding those winds and those waves, that have been stirred up by greed and lust, is Communism. And the Devil and his angels are riding with them.

The world is speedily ripening in iniquity. The floods of destruction cannot long be withheld. Only the direct command of God is momentarily controlling those destroying angels, for already has the edict been given: "See that you hurt not the trees, nor the grass, nor any green thing until the servants of God are sealed in their foreheads." (Rev. 7:2-3-)

This is repeated and verified in Revelations, chapter nine and verses one to six, as follows: "And the fifth angel sounded, and I saw a star fall from heaven to the earth; and to him was given the key of the bottomless pit.

"And he opened the bottomless pit; and there arose a great smoke out of the pit as the smoke of a great furnace; and the sun and the air were darkened by reason of the smoke of the pit.

"And there came out of the smoke locusts upon the earth: and unto them was given power as the scorpions of the earth have power.

"And it was commanded them that they should not hurt the grass of the earth, neither any green thing, but only those men which have not the seal of God in their foreheads.

"And to them it was given that they should not kill them, but that they should be tormented five months, and the torment was as the torment of a scorpion when he striketh a man.

"And in those days shall men seek death and shall not find it; and shall desire to die, and death shall flee from them."

After this period of suffering and peril, which will be permitted for the sole purpose of giving the wicked another chance, the end will come speedily. This end is not the annihilation of the world, as many have supposed. It will be the end of Lucifer's reign—the end of wickedness and evil and the suffering which goes with transgression. And then will it be thoroughly understood that it does not "take all kinds of people to make up a world."

"And the loftiness of men shall be bowed down and the haughtiness (pride) of men shall be made low: and the Lord alone shall be exalted in that day.

"And the idols he shall utterly abolish.

"And they shall go into the holes of the rocks, and into the caves of the earth, for the fear of the Lord, and for the glory of his majesty, when He ariseth to shake terribly the earth.

"In that day shall man cast his idols of silver and his idols of gold, which they have made each one for himself to worship, to the moles and to the bats:

"To go into the clefts of the rocks and into the tops of the ragged rocks for fear of the Lord, and for the glory of his majesty when He ariseth to shake terribly the earth.

"Cease ye from men, whose breath is in his nostrils; for wherein is he to be accounted of?" (Isa. 2:17-22). This command to cease giving your support to men, but to God only is the command to cease trusting in the arm of flesh, but go to God that you might KNOW Him!

"And the kings of the earth (the rulers and politicians), and the great men, and the rich men, and the chief captains, and the mighty men, and every bondman, and every freeman, hid themselves in the dens and in the rocks of the mountains:

"And said to the mountains and rocks, Fall on us

and hide us from the face of him that sitteth upon the throne, and from the wrath of the lamb.

"For the great day of his wrath is come; and who shall be able to stand?" (Rev. 6:15-17).

After the sun has been darkened and moon turned to blood and the wicked will have been given a brief period in which to repent, there will come greater destructions and perils than this world has ever before beheld.

Instead of darkness there will be a day of great heat in which the trees and grass and the green vegetation will be burned and shriveled to a crisp. "The moon will be as bright as the sun and the sun will be seven times brighter than seven days." It will be forty-nine times brighter and forty-nine times hotter than any ordinary day. (Isa. 30:26).

In that day the wicked, or those who have sinned too greatly to repent, "will lift up their voices and curse God, and die!" And in that day the wicked will be taken from the earth, for as promised from the beginning, "The meek shall inherit the earth!" "His spirit will be poured out upon all flesh," And those who are not purified cannot abide the day!" Those who have only polluted and defiled this beautiful world with their evils and greeds and lusts and whoremongering and murders will no longer be permitted to remain here. And even then, in His great mercy God will only remove them to other spheres or realms where they can "pay the uttermost farthing" for their rebellions and evils, and will be prepared finally to be released, with a chance of new beginnings, but with a memory of their old failures upon them.

Those who have not only sinned but have fought Light and Truth, and thus indirectly God, will become extinct. For them will come the second death, the death of the spirit, as they are consumed by the glory of His outpouring Light.

Every adversary of truth and of righteousness, every evil-doer, every individual on this earth, who has turned aside for a thing of naught, is even now being gathered into bundles, or groups, for the tares are being separated from the wheat—not the wheat from the tares, as in previous times. This reverse procedure is in itself a strange act and most unusual, for never before has this taken place. Always the great movements of the past have been to gather up the righteous—not the wicked. The movement of Hitler was to gather up the wicked and to lead them out to destruction. The movement of Communism is to gather up the wicked, or those who have forfeited their right to their free-agency by becoming too passive. Here in America they are being gathered likewise into ways and avenues that will bring their downfall speedily and swiftly, and they realize it not.

The righteous are the ones who have learned to love, to listen to His voice, and to obey that voice. They are the ones who are perfecting, within themselves, that New Song of praise and love and gratitude. These are the ones who have exalted their love and developed the power of their faith until they are "filled with Light and will soon comprehend all things" for they are being prepared to have this power of light and knowledge and complete truth opened unto them.

When that divine, holy Light has been developed and brought forth from within, until it not only fills the hearts and souls, but every cell and fibre of their bodies and the tissues of their minds, that Light will become apparent to those who are spiritually advanced enough to behold it. That Light will be visible in their foreheads, or on their brows. This is the seal of God that has been promised. His seal is always Light.

At first only those, who are themselves righteous, will be able to discern that seal in others. However, before the work is completed, "All men will be able to discern between the righteous and the wicked, saith your God." (Malachi 3:18). And there is no power in existence that can fake that seal. It is radiantly beautiful. And glory be to him who wears it.

The destroying angels are waiting under that strict command, at the present time, to withhold their hands, "until the saints are sealed."

The great work of the NOW is to help in bringing forth that Light, by humbly assisting the righteous to place that seal upon themselves as they glorify God in a new devotion of increasing love and gratitude.

This is the work of Reason and I, along with others, have been ordained to help fulfill.

These mighty ones, and all you who are now preparing yourselves in love and faith, will have that seal placed upon your foreheads as you bring forth that triumphant, Celestial Song of everlasting power into its full measure of divine harmony, for these released vibrations are the great Christ Light. This Song contains the full vibratory glory of His exquisite, powerful Light that fulfills all things. And when it is established permanently within one's entire being, then will that seal be visible, to the righteous and in the righteous.

Love and praise and worship and adore and give thanks that God has sent His angels to stand beside you until "your calling and election is made sure!" Or until you no longer doubt, for the command is: "Doubt not! Fear not! But rejoice evermore!"

In your hands will be placed power such as you have never dreamed of possessing. When the catastrophies come, and they will come speedily, you will have the power of the Almighty upon you. And with outstretched arms you will be able to assist in holding back the complete annihilation of the earth. You will have the power, in that day, to rebuke and command even death—to ease suffering and to glorify God in your every action for your lives will become sanctified unto Him as you become servants in His hands in every deed. You will have the power to protect your loved ones, if so be they will permit. The power of God will be so mighty upon you you will be able to walk through the fires of a perishing world and help preserve it from annihilation.

"The great and mighty day of the Lord" is **at** hand!"

It is the day in which, "One mighty and strong will be sent to set the house of God in order." *Such a one would not be needed to be sent if everything was not out of order.* There are those who are mistakenly anticipating that one of the most holy, divine ones from on High will be sent to approve and associate with them. In this hope they err greatly. "That one mighty and strong" will not come to approve and to exalt. *"That one"* will hold the sword of rebuke up in condemnation. "That one mighty and strong" will remove the proud and the arrogant. He will rebuke those who are out of order and who lack in love and humility and who in their self-righteousness have failed to either contact God or to seek Him. "These are the ones who have professed to know His name, and have not—and who have blasphemed against Him in the midst of His house."

"And in that day men will pray day and night for deliverance!" For only as men humble themselves in great and mighty prayer can the house of God possibly be set in order. For then only will they be prepared to listen—and hence—to learn. With humbled hearts and cleansed souls, those who are spared, will covenant anew, with God, to serve only Him and to obey His laws of truth and righteousness.

"Verily, Verily, I say unto you, darkness covereth the earth, and gross darkness the minds of the people. And *ALL* flesh has become corrupt before my face.

"Behold, vengeance cometh speedily upon the inhabitants of the earth, a day of wrath, a day of mourning, and of lamentation; and as a whirlwind it shall come upon all the face of the earth, saith the Lord.

"And upon my house shall it begin, and from my house shall it go forth, saith the Lord.

"First among those among you, saith the Lord, who have professed to know my name and have not known me, and have blasphemed against me in the midst of my house, saith the Lord." (D. & C. 112)

"For the head went down to the feet, for down to the feet ran the wheel and that which was a sign upon it." (23 Ode of Solomon)

Such will be the beginning of destructions and such will be the ending as the earth is cleansed of all unrighteousness. And those unworthy to live upon it will be given opportunities to repent and to reform. And to those who desire there will be opened up new avenues of opportunity, if so be they are prepared to make use of them.

But you noble ones, who are sealed, or who are being sealed with that holy seal of Light, for you is awaiting all that your beloved hearts could ever dream of possessing, "for eye hath not seen, nor ear heard, neither hath it entered into the heart of man the great things which God hath prepared for them that love Him."

You, great and noble ones, will continue upon this earth to help glorify the world. You will be assistants, under Jesus Christ, Lord of Lords, and King of kings to help establish permanent peace. And in love and under a reign of sublime beauty will an era of righteousness and peace be established. And blessed are you who are called to help establish it.

You, who carry this glorious Seal of God within your foreheads, are chosen indeed. You are the ones who, through your pure devotion, high spiritual thoughts and divine adoration have opened your hearts and minds to the full outflowing of His quickening Spirit as it is being released upon all your flesh. You noble ones have responded to the outpouring of that Celestial Christ Light, as your own love and devotion have brought it forth from within to fill your entire beings. When you are filled with this Light that "all-seeing, spiritual eye," within your foreheads will be opened to comprehend all things. And when that sacred, spiritual eye is opened, by the holy Light of Christ, the "Seal of God" is established. And no person on this earth can receive the glory of this divine blessing if he is *too sealed* in his own narrow, dogmatic, orthodoxed beliefs and conformity. This Seal of God can only be given to those who have opened their soul completely to His directing and brought forth that Light of Christ from within so that it is no longer a rejected factor.

"The Kingdom of Heaven" or the "Kingdom of Oranus" or "expansion" must first be opened wide from within to the great outpouring of His Holy Light in order for that Light to fill one's being and his heart and his mind. Only an unsealed mind can possibly receive that divine, holy Seal of God upon the forehead. One must be willing to test and "to prove all things" before he can receive of that dynamic, beneficial power of God's Spirit as it is poured out in increasing glory upon the inhabitants of the earth. Under the influence of this great out-pouring the righteous will become more righteous, more enlightened and better prepared for that great Seal to be placed upon their brows.

Those who are completely sealed and bound by their own beliefs and traditions will remain blind and unenlightened. Those who are completely evil will become more so under the impact of His Spirit, as it is poured out upon their flesh, until they will finally be consumed by it—"and become extinct."

You blessed ones, you who are opened and re-sponding to His outflowing Light, Come! Prepare yourselves speedily in love and praise and gratitude, to take your places in that which is to come! For so has God commanded me to write.

"Then shall the righteous shine forth as the sun in the kingdom of their Father, who hath ears to hear let him hear," proclaimed Jesus Christ, Son of the Living God." (Matt. 13:43).

And the time is at hand!

*(The sun to be darkened: Isa. 24:23; Joel 2:10; 3:15; Mat. 24:29; Mark 13:24; Luke 23:45.)

THE DIVINE WILL OF GOD

Chapter XV

The following is a conspectus of some of the truths that have been explained in these books, which God has commanded me to write. This brief summary is given here to refresh the memory of each individual upon the dynamic highlights that mark His divine Pathway to the very stars.

The first requisite to even begin to travel that "Straight and Narrow Way" of glory which Christ gave is the ability to *believe,* or to *be* and *live* according to the teachings He revealed. He left the perfect map to that glorious Way of Life, which so few find, not that it is not plainly marked, but because so very few are desirous of changing themselves that they might KNOW. In order to develop even the power to *believe* it is necessary that one *be* and *come* to the point where his vision is lifted to behold "the glory of God." At least one must comprehend, in a measure, the desirability of a path and a goal so gloriously divine. One must *be* the *attitude* of every righteous instinct until they are thoroughly developed and established within. As one's own highest spiritual qualities are developed the evil, negatious ones are overcome automatically. This is the "overcoming" so necessary for fulfilment. As one fulfills the greatness locked within himself and releases it he will soon "find his calling and election made sure." Those divine, coveted qualities will become his own without either strife or difficulty. And he will become them—his very self—the great spiritual self of his own being.

It is not evil to believe that perfection is possible, and for man to strive for it, for so commanded Jesus Christ. And no commandment was ever given that did not contain the complete power of its own fulfilment. This work contains the vision of perfection as the ultimate goal of man. This does not mean just a state of mere mortal perfection, as one without power, accepts and acknowledges and occasionally practices "the Golden Rule," which is the highest *mortal law*. This perfection includes the law of the angels—then the laws of God as the complete, comprehensive adherence to Christ's command is fulfilled: "Be ye therefore perfect, even as your Father in heaven is perfect!"

Any who will only make the effort to *prove* the laws He proclaimed by LIVING them will KNOW of their power and their truth and will be granted "the Life more Abundant"—"even Life Eternal!"

As one exerts the effort to LIVE the laws he will grow into the dynamic powers of perfection and will automatically "overcome" his own weaknesses and evils. His own weaknesses, whether inherent or self-developed, along with all mortal inclinations will be gradually discarded like repulsive, worn out rags.

The knowledge that death is not only unnecessary but a shameful experience is at first startling. Then, as one begins to *live* Christ's laws the deeper understanding of His precepts become embossed in clear radiance. One realizes fully that Christ came to earth to reveal the keys of overcoming death. He informed the world that "death would be the last enemy to be overcome." And man has sat back indolently expecting Christ to come and do that overcoming for him. This is because none have *lived his laws* that they might know of their truth and their power.

Each individual, as he exerts himself to begin to *live* His laws, that he might *know,* that divine, holy pathway of "overcoming" will unfold before him. As he progresses onward and upward he "grows from grace" or from virtue to virtue, he "fulfills all the laws of righteousness." "The nearer man approaches perfection, the clearer are his views and the greater are his enjoyments, *until he overcomes the evils of his life,* and loses every desire for sin, and like the ancients, arrives at the point of faith where he is wrapped in the power and glory of his Maker and is caught up to dwell with Him!" And as one fulfills this law of continual progress and develops into this degree of righteousness *death is automatically over-come* by that individual.

Death was never instigated by God. It was per-mitted, after the great transgression so "that man could not go on living forever in his sins." If men were permitted to go on living forever, in their sins and their blindness, the accumulation of suffering and distress and anguish would become intolerable and completely unbearable. Suffering is caused by the transgressing of men. Suffering is not caused by God. Death was permitted as a release from the accumulation of evils and continued wickedness and impossible suffering created thereby.

"By sin came death!" When sin is overcome, in any life, then death will also be conquered, for it is the last enemy to be overcome in any life.

"But every one follows his own wicked lusts: *having taken up an unjust and wicked envy, by which DEATH first came into the world.*" (I. Clement, 2:5—Lost Books of the Bible).

In the record of Nicodemus, XVIII: 5:6 (ibid), is given this revealing information: *"O Satan, prince of all evil, AUTHOR OF DEATH, and source of all pride,* thou shouldest first have inquired into the crimes of Jesus of Nazareth, and then thou wouldst have found that he was guilty of no fault worthy of death.

"Why didst thou venture, without either reason or justice, to crucify him, and have brought down to our regions a person innocent and righteous, and therefore hast lost all the sinners, impious and unrighteous persons in the world?"

And from the most ancient records of the earth stands forth this divine proclamation: "On him who overcomes sin, death has no claim!"

And as stated in the scriptures: "The wages of sin is death!"

There is another reference to this power of overcoming death given in what is known as "THE WORD OF WISDOM!" This is offered by God for the physical, temporal and spiritual welfare of all who will live by it. There is also given the promise that they who obey it and keep all his commandments shall be delivered from death. In this revelation is an injunction to refrain from tobacco and all strong drinks; to eat meat sparingly, in other words, not to defile the body by permitting the sense of taste to become a gluttonous dictator. The revelation is followed by the breathtaking promise first given by Isaiah, the prophet, and is as follows: "And all saints who remember to keep and do these sayings, *walking in obedience to the commandments* (or the laws of Christ), shall receive health in their navel, marrow in their bones; and shall run and not be weary; and walk and not faint. They shall receive treasures of knowledge, even hidden treasures. And, *I, the Lord, give unto them a promise that the destroying angel shall pass by them as the children of Israel, and not slay them.*"

There are many who fulfill the first part of this revelation in strict, almost fanatic conformity then go on to hate their brother, cheat their neighbor, mistreat their wives, domineer over their children and otherwise break all the loving, tender, most powerful teachings of Christ's divine kingdom. These who do not accept and live ALL the laws of right-eousness are deceiving themselves. They are only wearing the robes of self-righteousness. And those robes of self-righteousness are most deceptive. On that great day that affected, artificial covering will melt away and be dissolved back into the pride from which it was spun. And the shame and the nakedness of those who have been satisfied with the outward show of things will stand forth horrified and humiliated. Then will they slink away completely condemned by their own sins made apparent.

The living of the divine, holy laws of righteous-ness is far beyond the mere professing of them. The difference is as great as the brilliance of noonday compared to the deep darkness of midnight. One must LIVE the laws of profound beauty and un-limited power in order to fulfill the commands He gave, and hence *prove* them.

The fulfilling of the laws of righteousness is the only way one can possibly receive "The Life More Abundant" or prove his love for Christ. "If ye love me you will keep my conmmandments!" And, as John quoted the Master: "I am come that they might have life and have it more abundantly." (John 10:10). This was the purpose of Christ's coming, to break the bands of death by revealing the laws

by which death could be overcome by every child
of earth.

Christ's whole earthly mission was to bear witness
of, and to bestow this precious "Life more Abundant" upon those who were willing to fulfill the
laws of its divine glory. The very keys of "Life
Eternal" He held out to a dying world—a world
enshrouded in death as each individual plodded his
slow, dreary way to the grave.

The pure laws Christ gave, of love and tenderness
contain the pattern of each man's overcoming as he
casts aside the binding claims of the flesh and of
mortality. His way is the inner way of purification
and of perfection as the inside of the cup (of man)
is cleansed.

Christ said: "If thou wilt *enter into life* keep the
commandments." He also proclaimed, "If you love
me, keep my commandments!" There are so many
who profess their love for Him though they have
never exerted the least effort to LIVE His divine
laws of love and of forgiveness and tender service,
indicated in that precious Sermon on the Mount.
None have sought to BE-COME the BE-ATTI-
TUDES He recommended for fulfilment.

The information has been unfolded in this work
that as one learns to blend his will with the *Divine
Will of God* all things will be fulfilled in him, for
in the Will of God is all perfection held. To comprehend fully the blending of one's will with the

holy Will of God there must be another bit of information added.

There are many, who briefly scanning the law without yet having learned to live it, have attempted to cease working. Some have refused to make the least effort to support either themselves or their families with this blind, self-righteous excuse, "The Lord will provide!" "The Lord does provide!" He provides the earth and the fullness thereof for the benefit of mortal man. His great abundance is there for man to use as he learns to subdue the earth. God not only provides the earth, the soil, the sunshine and the water for the bringing forth, he provides the seasons for planting and harvesting. He provides man with the intelligence and the power to make use of the abundance He has provided. Man was meant to be active, creative and diligent. God does surely provide an abundance of all things but man is required to bring them forth until he has fulfilled *all* the laws of righteousness. Until, by his own exerted efforts he lifts himself into a higher status of spiritual advancement he is required to obtain that abundance, which the Lord provides, by his own efforts. Even in the Garden of Eden "Adam was required to dress and keep the garden." One may not be a farmer, nor need to be to gather for his use the great abundance which God has provided. There are industries and professions and businesses in which a man can serve and reap of the abundance which God has provided.

It is only as one fulfills *all* the laws of righteousness, which pertain to the Kingdom of God, that he will be able to use those higher laws of creation and bring forth from the universal "substance of things hoped for" the fulfilling of every need. In this higher law nothing is lacking and one is lifted or released from the laws of mammon and the need to labor for the things that perish. This is the perfect condition and one most desirable. With this law one can multiply the five loaves and three fishes, the oil in the tiny cruse, or he can fulfill instantly any need by his own praising law of gratitude. This is one of the powers of His kingdom, when one has found it. This law is every man's to use when he has obeyed the laws of righteousness.

But to fulfill this higher law, in which one *"no longer needs to labor for the things that perish"* one has to exert himself beyond anything a lazy, slothful, indolent person could ever dream of. He must "exercise great and mighty faith." And this type of exercise demands a rigid training of the mind and the heart and the soul. It is a road of discipline as one becomes a true disciple learning to bring his rambling thoughts, his wagging tongue, his every motion under complete control. This higher law of unspeakable power requires the complete renovation of every slothful, negligent, lazy, immature habit. It demands that one BE and LIVE every law of righteousness. And in the very effort of seeking to live these higher laws is a reward of continual outflowing satisfaction and increasing advancement.

And so as one learns to relinquish the need to

"labor for his daily bread" by exerting his every faculty of advancing splendor the same is true in learning to relinquish one's will to the divine will of God.

To relinquish one's will to the holy Will of God does not mean that one give up every desire, every hope of fulfilment and every personal effort to attain in a stupid state of dull inactivity, waiting for God to do the fulfilling for him. It is true that when "God unveils His face to any individual it will be in *God's own time* and in *His own way* and according to *His own Will*," and *that will be when the individual himself is completely purified and prepared.* When the individual is ready then IS *the time* that God will fulfill the great promise of His patient waiting. And each individual himself must do that work of preparation. He must prepare himself.

To blend one's will with the Will of God requires a knowledge of the Will of God. And here it must be made known—*and never be forgotten*: It is never God's Will that any child of His be a failure, a misfit, a miserable, unhappy, grubby mortal, without vitality or dreams or vision or hope. Any individual who weakly accepts any ugly, negatious, desolate, miserable, unprogressive, unsatisfactory existence, believing it is the Will of God, has never fulfilled that divine, glorious command "To lift his eyes to the glory of God, and to hold them single to that glory!"

As one fulfills this command to "hold his eyes single to the glory of God," he begins to comprehend the breathtaking splendor of God's holy Will and knows that in His Will is contained only his own perfection, his own shining splendor, his own divine fulfilment.

"For this is my work and my glory, to bring to pass the immortality and the eternal life of man!"

And there are those who nurture and cultivate their misery and unhappiness and their poverty in the evil, mistaken belief that it will bring them a greater reward in heaven. In this idea they err greatly. In Revelations it tells plainly that in the day of their resurrection that he who is filthy will be filthy still and *he that is unhappy will be unhappy still*. If you are miserable and unhappy in this life it is because you have not applied the laws of Christ nor exerted yourself enough to fulfill the wonder of their power and hence you have failed utterly to prove his promises, and heaven and the resurrection holds out no great rewards to such.

Blend your will with the Will of God and you will begin to comprehend the dynamic power of His desires for you, the unspeakable blessings He is holding out for you now—and forever. You will begin to comprehend the pattern of your own unfolding, the breathtaking glory of God's dynamic blessings which He WILLS to bestow upon you as soon as you are prepared to receive them.

As you begin to understand His Will you will also begin to comprehend the laws and the powers of creation and will know your part in helping to fulfill them. As you *live* the laws of His Will you will *know* of their truth and their power and you will develop your own power in fulfilling all things.

Of you it is required that "you lay hold of the BEST gifts" not just any old thing that is left over of talents or joys or substance. *You must "lay hold of the BEST gifts"—The very BEST!* Then you must hold those desires out to God, for His fulfilling. THIS IS HIS WILL! Of you it is required to exercise great and mighty faith by holding that request of your soul, in your mind, as you project the vision or pattern or diagram of it out to reflect its image upon the clear, *"still"* surface of that pool or mirror of liquid, glorious gold that has been tried in the fire. As you do this then only can the "Father do the works" of fulfilling. Of you it is required to hold your request forth "without doubting or wavering, for he that wavereth is like a wave of the sea driven by the wind and tossed. And let not that man think that he shall receive anything of the Lord." And he who sits back indolently, inactively permitting his hopes and desires to be erased and blotted out in the mistaken belief that he is blending his will with the Will of God is on the path to Spiritual death! Such will find himself sitting in his utter desolation of unfulfilled possibilities until he slowly ceases to exist.

It IS the "Father who doeth the works!" And "It *is* the Father who rewards you openly." But it is you who must become the powerful vehicle in which His divine power of fulfilling can operate. It is the Father who supplies those rays of radiant, limitless Light and Who has established the law by which they are converted into atoms as they are curled upon themselves by your exerted exercising of faith. It is your part, in the Will and plan of God, to begin to make use "of the substance of things hoped for" as you mirror out your righteous desires with all the energy and power you can possibly generate. *It is the Father Who provides* the material and the substance for that fulfilling.

Only as man begins to LIVE the laws of God, which are the laws of his own progress and fulfilment, can God begin to do His works of fulfilling glory. As one works with God *"The substance of things hoped for"* takes tangible form and fulfills every righteous desire of the soul of him who begins to LIVE the laws. "NOTHING IS IMPOSSIBLE" to him who believes! And everyone who believes will fulfill the laws of righteousness and will therefore use rightly the divine, holy laws of creation.

THIS IS THE WILL OF GOD!

And only by becoming a co-creator with God in the use of His holy laws can one possibly fulfill His Will or blend his own will into the divine Will of God.

As the key to His desire for you He has given this sacred information: "This is the Will of the Father, that you *believe* on Him Whom He has sent!" If you believe on Jesus Christ then you must also believe in His Light which He gave to abide in you. You must also bring that Light forth as you fulfill the laws of righteousness. And if you DO *believe* then you *must* begin to do the works which He did. This is His Will! You must *live the laws* that you

might KNOW of their truth and obtain the fullness
of their power.

THIS IS THE WILL OF GOD!

"Hold your eyes single to the glory of God!"
Keep your vision high! "Without vision the people
perish!" There is no power or strength or accomplishment in any individual who has not the power to
hold that vision.

To have "eyes single to the glory of God" has
been stressed in this work for a very definite reason.

The power of this statement, fulfilled, is boundless. It has many aspects and many approaches and
a continual unfolding of possibilities and results and
powers as one begins to "take hold of it as one of
the best gifts" and lives by it.

This dynamic, glorious, powerful bit of information is stated in its fullness as follows: "And if
your eyes be single to my glory, your whole bodies
shall be filled with light, and there shall be no darkness in you; and that body which is filled with light
comprehendeth all things.

"Therefore, sanctify yourselves, that your minds
become single to God, and the days will come that
you shall see Him; for He will unveil His face unto
you, and it shall be in His own time, and in His
own way, and according to His own will.

"Remember *the great and last promise* which I
have made unto you; cast away your idle thoughts
and your excess of laughter far from you." The
greatest and the last promise to be fulfilled unto
those who are striving for perfection is to behold

the face of God. "And this is life eternal!" This is the greatest promise possible to give and the greatest one possible to receive.

Now, another meaning of this glorified revelation I am instructed to unfold. If one will take every bleak, unhappy, desolate, evil happening, every misfortune, every set-back, every sorrow and every ounce of suffering and dedicate them to the glory of God that individual's ability to transmute conditions into power will be fully achieved. Like Christ, he will have the power henceforth to take every dishonorable, polluted, shameful, tragic happening and condition and glorify them completely by his exulting praise and released adoration. This is how Christ exalted the blasphemy and the shame of His crucifixion into an everlasting blessing. This is how He conquered death!

No matter what comes into one's life it can be exalted and transmuted if the individual will accept it in praising love, with a released vibration of joyous gratitude for the glory of God. From the moment any individual can achieve this state of progress nothing evil can ever again touch his life, for "he will have overcome the evils of his life." "And all things will henceforth work together for his good!" Then follows the dynamic promise that "All things will become subject unto him, both in heaven and on earth, the Light and the life, the Spirit and the power—!"

No powers or promises are greater than these and

it is THE WILL OF GOD that man attain them, by living the laws which pertain to them.

As you hold to your vision of perfection and your desire of fulfilment, without doubting, "God will do the works" of fulfilling.

In this higher work you not only blend your will completely with the Will of God, you become a co-creator with Him as you begin to do the very works which Christ did—even greater works!

THIS IS THE WILL OF GOD!

MAN TRIUMPHANT

Chapter XVI

The law and the power of love is explained many times and in many ways throughout these volumes of God's revealing. One is commanded to *"pray with all the energy of heart"* that he might be possessed of this great love, that it will be well with him.

The sacred privilege and principle and the divine, breathtaking power of prayer is exalted into a vibrant glory of revelation as it takes on the supreme wonder of that "Narrow Way—the Path He trod—which so few find!"

The exquisite fullness of that superb, all-powerful command, "Let there be Light," as man makes use of that knowledge, is unspeakably beautiful!

The Church of the Firstborn is outlined and its principles of holiness are made known so that all those who desire might attain unto membership, if so be they will fulfill the laws, that they might be numbered among "The priests and priestesses of Golden Radiance!"

The status of becoming a "pillar in the temple of God" as one becomes a mighty, upholding power in supporting the whole, divine structure of eternal truth and Light is sublimely beautiful. One realizes that he was destined to become a very part of God's great Light and eternal truth as he reaches his own fulfilment.

Within these books is contained all that the mind of man can fathom at the present time and all that the soul of man can possibly desire in fulfilment, from the first vision of hope to the full bestowal of all gifts and power of creation.

The New Song, even that sacred, dynamic, Celestial Song of Creation is revealed in detail that all who desire might become living participants in that stupendous symphony of eternal glory.

And now, I am instructed to make clear the pathway of "overcoming." It is beautiful beyond anything man has ever dreamed and easy beyond belief. The whole pathway of glory is the road of discipline as one becomes a disciple. As one places himself under discipline he soon becomes an adept. Then as he continues he becomes a master. A master of what? He becomes the master of himself by mastering his own vibrations. Vibrations are the living forces of entities of his own creating. As he becomes aware of his dynamic creative powers they become subject unto him and he becomes the master.

"*Faith* is the substance (or material) of things *hoped* for, the evidence of things not seen." "If one is without hope he must need be in despair and despair cometh because of iniquity." When one learns to control the vibrations he normally releases through his dismays, set-backs, misfortunes or even unanalyzed thoughts and feelings, and holds himself in a state of inner calm and peace the evils and vicissitudes will be disarmed and become powerless. As one works to control vibrations he truly becomes a disciple for he places himself under the wondrous discipline of learning to control the very powers of creation. This indeed is mastery. This is the evolving from the man kingdom into the God kingdom. This is the beginning of divinity.

"Hope" is the great beacon of Lighted glory which is so necessary in order to have a happy, successful life of eternal achievement. "Hope" is the voice of *Promise*. It is the guiding beacon that will forever light the Way of him who will follow its sacred leading and guard it from the engulfing vibrations of evils and despairs. Any promise or *hope* which an individual is led to cherish in his heart is an individual revelation or promise that can become his own. It will all be fulfilled unto him, and more, regardless of what it is he is led to desire, if that hope or desire contained within his heart is noble and pure.

Only the eternal, unwavering, creative power of "hope" can fulfill the desires of the heart. and only as "hope" is guarded and kept alive by the perfect control of one's own released vibrations, which are the off-spring of his thoughts and emotions intermingled, can *hope* complete the pattern or design of its own destiny. And only as one keeps his vibration in control can "hope" operate. And only *hope* can fulfill the yearning desires of the heart.

"Hope" is the pattern faith uses to produce realities. As *hope* becomes a living thing it will take form in the mind of an individual as clear and beautiful as a painting on a wall. The clearer are the details the more speedily and perfectly will the hope be fulfilled.

The full key to this dynamic, limitless power is held only by the individual who can control the vibrations which are hurled against him by outside conditions or forces or hate-filled individuals. But even more important, one must master and control every vibration which is released through his own being. One's own vibrations are his own creations. These released vibrations may be either destructive, deadly powers of unfathomable evil or they may be the very powers of godhood. When these vibrations of one's own creating are evil they become his enemies, and are of his own household. To rule one's own household in triumphant power one must realize that he is the head of his house as he exercises the authority of his mastery. He must fully comprehend the stupendous importance of his powers of divinely, exerted control as he uses them.

Only by the method of learning to control one's own vibrations in a divine harmony of glorious, inner peace can "hope" burn in an unwavering flame that must perfect the pattern of its own fulfilling.

"If any of you lack (hope or faith or) wisdom, let him ask of God Who giveth to all men liberally and upbraideth not; and it shall be given him. But let him ask in faith, without wavering, for he that wavereth is like a wave of the sea, driven by the wind and tossed.

"And let not that man think he shall receive anything of the Lord!"

Unwavering "hope" carries the attitude of expectancy. Expectancy is the perfect container held out for *faith* to fill full. "Hope" is the pattern. Expectancy is the container. And Faith is the substance out of which all desired things are formed.

Faith is hope carried to the point where despair cannot touch or mar or destroy the pattern held out for fulfilment.

"*Hope* promises all things and *Faith* fulfills them." Faith and *hope* are in a way synonymous. Faith is hope matured and made perfect, like a child grown into manhood.

"He who is *without hope* must needs be in despair. And despair cometh because of iniquity."

Despair comes when uncontrolled doubts, fears, despondency or any evil vibration is permitted to assail one and feed upon his strength and devour his radiant powers of glory. Dark, discouraging vibrations are completely demoralizing and will utterly destroy the perfect works of hope and faith. These intangible, elusive, almost unthought feelings of doubts and dismays and despondency are the flickering flames by which the true "gold is tried." These flames of despair, of inadequacy, of lack or fear or doubt may be only flickering little flashes. But there is no human being on the earth who is not tested and tried by them. These little, seemingly harmless flickers can leap instantly into a consuming conflagration that destroys the pattern hope held out in the divine container of expectancy.

This "pure gold that must be tried in the fire," is the spiritual gold of that reflecting mirror of fulfilment when one, through understanding, has learned to control the fire, using it solely for good. Fire has been one of mankinds greatest blessings when controlled and one of his greatest curses when it is permitted to go out of bounds. When a person, with powerful vibrations, uses them knowingly for good nothing is impossible. When one ignorantly permits destructive, evil vibrations to be released through himself he has placed himself within the fires of hell and realizes it not. And unless he begins to comprehend and to become the master he will be destroyed.

As one learns to study and understand vibrations he comprehends that they are the flickering, leaping flames of his own testing as he works toward mastery. As vibrations are mastered and used rightly they purify that inner gold of the spirit and it becomes perfected. These flickering flames of one's accepted or released vibrations could also be likened to "the waves of the sea," mentioned by Saint James. When evil, negative vibrations are permitted to dictate and take over that inner pool of gold, it, instead of becoming pure, and "stilled" as a mirror, becomes storm tossed, turbulent and a reflector of shattered hopes in its great disquietude. And so only the reflection of shattered fragments of the holy desire is reflected out to be fulfilled. "And let not that man think that he shall receive anything of the Lord."

As long as one is tossed emotionally by every dismaying, unhappy, disconcerting condition or vicissitude or thought that is out of tune with that "stilled" perfection of expectant hope, there can be no power of glorious fulfilling operative. It is not that God is unwilling to bestow all that is desirable, but the individual is unprepared to receive.

"Hope" is a sensitive, tender, delicate painting. It is a fragile picture. Hope is composed of a spiritual substance which depicts a glorious vision of promise, waiting for fulfilment. It is the blue-print of that which was meant to become. This etherial pattern must be safeguarded and appreciated. Doubts mar it. Unbelief or despair or despondency or negation can utterly destroy it. The vision, which "hope" is must be cherished and protected from all dismaying, depressing vibrations, from despair and from fear for they will destroy it utterly.

"Hope" is the spiritual formation of divine vision placed within the soul of man. It is composed of spirit matter and made permanent by the brush strokes of the vibrations used by the individual as he perfects the promises of God whispered into his heart. Only by the control of one's own vibrations can that celestial painting, formed by "hope," be made an everlasting reality. Only evil vibrations can destroy it. And only exalted, glorious vibrations can fulfill it.

Vibrations can be the glory of one's life if they are dynamic vibrations of living light which one permits to enter his being and then sends on out with ever more powerful energy directing their release in the complete glory of fulfilment. Vibrations can also be the evil of overwhelming darkness which bring the degredation of suicide, insanity or continuous misery and failure into one's life. Sordid, desolating vibrations are "the evils of one's life that must be overcome."

Bleak, desolate, hopeless vibrations are the invisible forces of existence which destroy "hope" or one's living promise of glory, leaving only a heap of burned-out, ugly ashes where the divine pattern was held, deep in the heart of man.

"As one overcomes the evils of his life (which are the negatious vibrations), and loses every desire for sin, he reaches the point of faith where he is wrapped in the power and glory of his Maker and is caught up to dwell with Him!" No saying ever revealed contains more truth or greater promise than this. The promise contained within it is so blinding in its glory few have been able to behold it.

To master vibrations, or the forces of life and death, it must be made apparent just what they are. So very few have ever comprehended them or even given them a thought simply because they cannot be seen by our physical eyes. They are the powerful, invisible forces of existence. They are the great realities. They are the cause of the things that are— and the things that will be.

Behind hate, resentments, hurt feelings, fears, jealousy and greed, along with all the other emotions of evils experienced by mankind, are the destructive powers of darkness and disease (dis-ease) and destitution and misery and death. These things are most real but the vibrations which are their cause have been ignored because they are invisible, intangible and immeasurable to mortal eyes and to the physical senses.

It is only by controlling vibrations that a release from drab, desolate mortal existence can be possible.

And contrary to the belief of those who have only a very vague understanding of vibrations, it is not so much the evil vibrations of others being hurled against us that are so devastating. It is those vibrations which we release within ourselves that toss us and distress us and destroy us and our pattern of "hope" with its promise of fulfilment. The vibrations of others can only effect us to the degree in which we permit ourselves to be influenced by them.

It is only our own reactions to the actions or vibrations or words of others that their influence can find a response in us. There are, of course, those whom we contact in life who are completely repellent, depressing and almost deadening in their dull, unanimated unaliveness. And there are those who lift our spirits to the very skies even as they brush by us in passing.

The dark, negative, depressing vibrations, or the hate-filled vicious, degenerate ones, which others send out, need only be understood in order for us to ignore or conquer them without stress or dismay.

Every individual has the power to instantly transmute any evil vibration, which is sent to him, by translating those vibrations into living rays of light and then returning them. On the wings of love and blessing all dark vibrations can be instantly exalted, transmuted and returned to the sender. As returned rays of light they can heal the sender or destroy him according to his acceptance or rejection of them. If he fights against them he is "fighting against the light" which has been increased a thousand fold by your having transmuted it. If he accepts these, his own vibrations, returned to him in living power he can be healed. Within this knowledge is contained the full meaning of that divine, beautiful command: "Pray for your enemies. Pray for those who despitefully use you or persecute you!" Each person has the power of divine healing thus held in the fulfilling reality of that hither-to-fore uncomprehended command.

You indeed have the power of divine healing within you as you return the vibrations of an enemy to him in love and understanding. It is up to him to accept those glorified, transmuted vibrations or to reject them. They are his own. If they are accepted that individual can be instantly healed of his warring hates and deadly evils. If he rejects your proffered blessing of living light his own vibrations will turn back upon him in a manner that will bring annihilation. This is no concern of yours. You are to love, to bless and to rejoice in the power of foregiveness which you have offered.

These great forces of transmutation, sent out by your love and released light and forgiveness are unspeakable. They can never be used in mere words, or be expressed in any spoken language. They are released powers and are dynamic beyond words.

Then there are the vibrations that will seek, at a moment of unawareness, to take over your life. These black waves of fear, dismay, desolation, despondency or dismal doubts are hurled out from the kingdom of the Prince of Darkness and his rampant legions of screaming, destructive forces of warring, negation and defiant rebellion. These are the most deadly ones and must be understood.

These vibrations of evil are forever being hurled against humanity from the Nether Regions seeking to enslave, destroy, to injure and to molest and retard the progress of man. And it is these vibrations that are the most intangible, elusive and detrimental. One can be on a high pinnacle of peace or tri-

umphant, joyous ecstasy, then without cause or
reason he can feel that he is sitting on the very brink
of despair and hopelessness. It is these vibrations
that inflict suicide and insanity and failure upon the
distressed mortals of mankind, those who have never
been taught about their influences nor powers nor
know how to combat them. These are the evils of
the great ignorance—or darkness.

There are thousands of defeated, frustrated individuals who have yielded their minds, their lives
and often their souls to help bolster the terrifying
legions of the realms of destruction. They do not
realize that within themselves is the power to combat such darkness and such abhorent evils. One has
but to request that the divine Light, locked within
himself, "Stand Forth!" Or if he will only give forth
that dynamic, silent command, "Let there be Light"
God can indeed do the works—of overcoming.

Thus it is within the power of every child of earth
to use that divine Light of Christ to bring a full
measure of peace into his life when apparently there
is no peace in all existence. And as one learns to
hold himself within this wall of peace the vibrations
of darkness are dissipated and dispelled—they are
conquered—even transmuted forever into light.

Any individual who begins to use these powers
of transmutation soon becomes *adept* in their use.
And thus it is possible for him to advance speedily
into true mastery.

At first this takes practice. The effort is not in
using the divine, inherent powers God vested in man,

but in *remembering* to use them so that instant control might be accomplished. And it is practice that makes perfect.

This is the work of a neophyte or a disciple as he places his own thoughts and reactions under discipline, guarding every emotion and every vibration of his life.

This is not at all difficult. It only takes a very few such triumphant experiences to make one *adept* in the use of the dynamic control necessary for mastery. Automatically when one has fully comprehended the issues involved and learned to subdue or command vibrations he indeed becomes the master.

This understanding goes beyond thought control. It reaches into and takes hold of the very forces of life itself. "And all things become subject unto him, both the Life and the Light; the Spirit and the Power," etc.

Learn to control vibrations as you exercise your God-given rights and the very secrets of life and glory will become yours to use for the benefit of a world.

So have I been instructed to bear witness. And so can every child of earth prove for himself the truth of these dynamic, eternal promises of Almighty God as he takes hold of them with his mind and lives accordingly.

———

A neophyte is a disciple or one who begins to discipline himself in his own reactions.

An adept is one who becomes adept or proficient

in controling the vibrations which are hurled at him from without.

A master is one who has gained perfect control of all the vibrations which he himself releases. Such a one becomes powerful indeed for power will be placed in his hands. And only such, trained, worthy ones could possibly be prepared to handle it.

To more speedily be able to use the dynamic vibrations of unlimited power one can begin by practicing the divine and holy art of sending forth the vibrations of pure, compassionate, understanding love. Love is the vehicle in which the Light is carried.

Send love through your eyes to enfold and bless in a caressing warmth of holiness all that your vision beholds. Practice constantly sending love through your tones as you speak. Send love through every cell and fiber of your being until you actually become this love. Or, as an ancient prophet suggested: "Pray with all the energy of heart that you might be possessed of this love — that it might be well with you . . . ."

And again: "The Fruit of the Tree of Life is the love of God which is shed forth through the hearts of the children of men." If you would partake of the fruit of the Tree of Life and live forever, you must perfect the great love as you permit it to be shed forth through your heart. This is indeed "the fountain of living waters—which if a man drink thereof he need never die!"

As one seeks ever to increase the flow of love through his own heart the supply increases until it reaches out to bless and heal a world—then goes on to embrace eternity.

Perfect love is not only the reality of "the life more abundant" it IS that life. And as one perfects this love it becomes "Life Eternal." Within it is contained the power to overcome death. "The wages of sin is death." "The wages of overcoming is Life eternal!" And "Death is the last enemy to be overcome." Uncontrolled vibrations, which are the sired entities of thoughts and emotions, are the first enemy. Death is the last one and will be automatically overcome as the first one is conquered and brought into subjection.

The unspeakable power to banish and overcome death is not only held in the controlling of vibrations but in increasing the power of the righteous ones. And love generates the most powerful vibration of all. The vibrations of love contains power unspeakable. And every individual can develop and use these unspeakable vibrations for his own release from decay, failure, stagnation and death.

These are the keys of "Life and Light and of Spirit and of Power" which become subject unto those who first become neophytes under discipline, then go on to become adept in the glory of perfect mastery. This is the point where "all things truly become subject unto him, both in heaven and on earth!"

———————

The great Light of everlasting power, which holds all progress enfolded in its embrace, is stimulated

and brought forth through one's own thought actions. It becomes a permanent reality by continued
awareness.

The whole road of glory is traveled by each individual as he begins to accept and fulfill his own purification instead of rushing after others and clinging
to their garments, seeking to be carried along on
their strength. Whatever degree of righteousness
any individual has achieved others may achieve
through their own efforts.

This great, creative Light of eternal power is
stimulated, increased and brought forth, it is true,
through one's own thought actions just as lusts,
greeds, hates and jealousies are stimulated and developed by one's own thought actions.

The evil, degenerate books that are being fos-
tered upon the children of men and unselective ignorant, immoral adults hold all the powers of destruction in their vileness. And those who produce them
are worse than the Hitlers of the world. The Hitlers,
reaching for personal power, destroy only the bodies
of men. But those who produce works to stimulate
lust, either by books, pictures or in the fields of en-
tertainment are assisting in the destruction of the
souls of men. Because they are pleased with such
things they think they are pleasing the public. Only
those of the lowest moral caliber are pleased. The
majority are sickened and revolted. Yet the issue is
so subtle and so evil the world stands by in a helpless, inadequate manner of almost stupified inactivity.

Unless those responsible for such laxness and all

self-respecting, decent human beings rise up to give
battle the whole world will be rocked by the vibrations that are being generated by the greed of individuals who are growing fat on the perverted powers of man. These individuals who are responsible
for this growing perversion have become monsters.
They are classified as completely sub-mortal or sub-
human as they traffic in the souls of the children of
men to satisfy their greed for money and luxury.
And their gains will perish with them and their souls
shall wreathe in the hell of their own regrets.

One more thought I am instructed to add to this
work before it is closed and sealed. As one learns
to control vibrations he becomes powerful. The
Christ, or Light vibrations of love and singing praise
and spontaneous, adoring gratitude is the path that
leads one to the very throne of God. As one practices
sending forth these vibrations and continues to send
them out he becomes the love and the light, for "he
becomes that which he seeks to interpret."

As soon as any individual has prepared himself,
or purified himself, he will be contacted by those in
higher authority. He will not need to seek them.
They will be sent to him and he will be lifted up
and will be ordained of God when he is thoroughly
prepared. Then will he be sent forth to fulfill all
things in a dynamic power of everlasting glory. And
all things will become subject unto him. The Light
he has generated within himself becomes his own
and he becomes IT. The gift of Life, which is in-

tensified and made perfect will be fully comprehended. It will also become his to command. The
Spirit and the power become his to use for the glory
of God and for the benefit of man. And "nothing
will be impossible to him!"

And now I speak a tender word to those of you
who have read the records God instructed me to
write, and who have accepted them. As you continue to lend your energies and your power to be-lieve
these sacred, pure, holy principles of righteousness
you are on that journey of perfection that will fulfill every promise and bestow the fulness of His Light.

And know that I shall be looking forward eagerly
to meeting you when your testing is over and you
have proved yourself worthy of all that is possible
to receive.

Your loving, devoted sister,
Annalee Skarin